Spirit of Nepean

D. Aubrey Moodie

with Andrea M. McCormick

Copyright D. Aubrey Moodie, 2003
ISBN 0-9733355-0-5
Design and production: Deanna Fenwick
Printed by: Motion Creative Printing, Carleton Place, Ontario
Front Cover Photo by: Dixie Photography

Contents

Dedication

To my wife Ella
for her love and support

Preface

One evening in the autumn of 2000, I sat down to watch the local television news. I was particularly interested in the broadcaster's account of how Nepean's growing community of Barrhaven came to be. I was incredulous. The story was full of errors.

For years, close friends had urged me to write my memoirs, but I had yet to appreciate its value. Immediately following that broadcast, a delegation came to the house to encourage me, once again, to share my memories.

John Monaghan, a neighbour and descendant of one of Nepean's pioneer families, was particularly vocal. "Tell us what we don't know about Nepean, Aubrey," he said.

I thought about what he had said and decided it was time to share a collection of stories about the challenges I faced and the milestones I reached as a person, as a municipal leader and as a volunteer. This is not a definitive history. In fact, some may find this story has familial undertones. That, in fact, is an accurate reflection of the way we worked together, striving for the best for the community. The stories underscore the spirit of Nepean and how it prevailed as we transformed a rural township, with a population of 2,500 with little or no services, into one of Ontario's fastest growing communities in the 1960's and one of Canada's best today. In fact, the unprecedented growth we managed in the 1960's would never again occur in Nepean's history.

Communities grow into healthy and vibrant places because of people who take the time to care and to get involved. That's what will make the difference as we go forward into the 21st century. Knowing from whence you have come can help make that journey forward just a little smoother.

Once you leave politics, most assuredly, memories of your contributions fade with the passage of time. That's the reality of politics. Unfortunately some of the lessons learned along the way are left to be re-learned.

As I reflect, I believe Nepean has been fortunate to have had the right kind of leaders at the right time. For my part, the creation of the development charge provided the financing we needed and set the stage for affordable growth. But, our first task was to re-establish services that disappeared in the 1950 annexation by the City of Ottawa. We lost our police department and our fire department, the health unit, staff, and 18,000 of our 20,000 residents. Not one of the remaining major roads was paved and our business core was virtually wiped out. We worked with the Provincial Government to take advantage of every available grant and subsidy to ensure Nepean Township became one of Ontario's fastest growing municipalities.

At one point, no further development in Nepean was possible without funds to construct a sewage treatment plant. A plan came to me in the middle of the night – it was a brand new method of financing municipal infrastructure and a first in Ontario: development charges. The developers agreed to pay a lot levy for each new residential unit to cover the costs of constructing the sewage treatment plant. Use of lot levies or development charges, as they are known today as a method to pay for capital costs resulting from development or redevelopment, became common practice across Ontario. For example, contributions from development charges and subdividers of $7.7 million in 1999 and $10.6 million in 1998 were listed as sources of financing in the City of Nepean's 1999 Consolidated Financial Statement.

The next Reeve, Andrew Haydon, was the architect. He created the program for growth and its sustainability. His significant capital spending program was eventually tempered by launching the pay-as-you-go program in which money was set aside in reserve funds and used when expenses were incurred. His beloved Nepean Sportsplex became a landmark and his foresight in preserving green space for public use was legendary for its time. His were true community accomplishments.

Andy Haydon's legacy was enriched by Mayor Ben Franklin who stead-fastly maintained the pay-as-you-go program. His was a program of sound financial management in which fundamental infrastructure such as roads and sewers were repaired before more expensive rehabilitation was required which extended the life cycle. His signature is evident in the construction of "people" places such as: Ben Franklin Place – home to City Hall, the outdoor skating rink, Nepean Central Library and Centrepointe Theatre – the Minto Sports Field, the Nepean Seniors' Lawn Bowl and proactive water quality environmental initiatives such as state of the art stormwater management.

Nepean's last Mayor Mary Pitt had the untenable task of fending off what was to be the last and final threat to the municipality known as Nepean. In the name of amalgamation, lower costs and affordable services, Nepean became a part of the new City of Ottawa in 2001. History will ultimately define the success of the amalgamation. But will the spirit of Nepean survive?

My story can't be separated from the stories of Andy Haydon, Ben Franklin and Mary Pitt. While I can't tell their stories, I believe there are links and lessons to be shared. My life, truly, has been one of lifelong learning. Those lessons came from many sources – my grandparents' journey across the ocean, my hard-working parents, my family, my church, and my days growing up on a farm, life during the Great Depression, and my political friends and challengers.

I don't know if history will prove I was a good strategist or a great bluffer. My success was the result of listening to and learning from the opinions of others, appointing excellent staff, and having our citizens elect good Councils. We thrived because we had well-motivated, civic-minded Councillors who brought strong business and professional skills to the Council table.

Throughout my life, I have been surrounded by many friends, neighbours and colleagues who worked hard to help me make dreams come true. For that, I am eternally grateful.

I also have been blessed with loving parents, a fine family and most of all, my wife Ella who has been my biggest supporter during our 70 years of married life together. I owe my success, in large part, to her.

This story is my way of acknowledging the many, many people who made Nepean one of the best communities in Canada. They were and are bonded together by a sense of unity, family and fortitude – the very words emblazoned on Nepean's Coat of Arms. It is also a challenge to you and to those to come to embrace the spirit of Nepean by recognizing what needs to be done and having the will to work together for the good of the community.

All the best,

D. Aubrey Moodie

Crossing the Ocean

Dougal Munroe Moodie, D. Aubrey Moodie's father, was born during the voyage across the Atlantic Ocean in 1850. Dougal was named after Dougal Munro, the ship's captain.

Our story begins in 1618, Dunfermline, Fifeshire, Scotland. Excerpts from The Annals of Our History published by my cousin, Frederick W. Moodie in 1923, provide a glimpse of the past, the voyage across the ocean, and the early pioneer days in Bells Corners. I am proud of my grandparents' life journey and the determination they had to seek out a new life and make it a success in a new land. Frederick's very detailed work describes the depression in Scotland and my grandparents' life after they decided to cross the ocean in 1850 – the same year in which the Town of Bytown and the Township of Nepean were incorporated.

By the time my grandparents arrived in Canada, settlement in Nepean Township had started in earnest. Communities began to spring up along Richmond Road, the link between the military depot established in Richmond in 1818 and Richmond Landing – the entry point for settlement, just below the Chaudiére Falls on the Ottawa River. Bytown, located in northeastern Nepean Township, came into being to support the construction of the Rideau Canal, initiated by Lt. Col. John By under orders from England. When completed in 1832, the Rideau Canal provided an alternate protected inland transportation route for food, supplies and ammunition between Bytown and Kingston. It met the military objective of creating a secure supply route when the vulnerability of the St. Lawrence River – the main supply route for goods coming into Upper Canada from Europe – became apparent during the War of 1812. Construction of the canal fuelled the local economy by providing work and cash to help pioneer families buy land. Bytown was incorporated as a town in 1850, as the City of Ottawa in 1855, as the capital of the Province of Ontario in 1857, and as the capital of the Dominion of Canada in 1867.

The relationship between Nepean Township and the City of Ottawa took on a new dimension. Nepean's future would be defined by Ottawa's status as the nation's capital, by the Federal Government's heightened desire to beautify Ottawa, and by the sporadic, vitriolic municipal debates arising out of the City of Ottawa's nine major land annexations of Nepean.

Ottawa's need for more assessment dollars, in order to pay for city services, helped to drive some city residents and businesses to rural or undeveloped areas to avoid paying taxes for services that they either didn't value or couldn't afford.

The 19th century economy thrived largely on the lumber industry and mixed farming consisting of wheat, hay and pork. Today, the Federal Government, the high technology industry, the agricultural industry, and the tourism industry create a diverse Ottawa economy. I have relied on Frederick Moodie's work to describe from whence we came.

Excerpts from *The Annals of Our History* by Frederick W. Moodie, 1923

➤ Several of the family attained honorable positions in the council of the burgh or town of Dunfermline, the birthplace of our family. From 1792 to 1807, James Moodie was Provost of Dunfermline and was a very excellent Mayor, and during the threatened invasion of Briton by Bonaparte, James Moodie was Lieutenant-Colonel of the Dunfermline Volunteer Corps.

➤ In the early history of Scotland, it was at one time the most important town of the nation and is ultimately connected with

Scotland's greatest kings, and was known as the Royal Burgh – it was chosen by King Malcolm III as his place of residence. Nearly all Scotland's kings, including Robert Bruce are interred here.

➤ Weaving was the principal industry of the town at this time, and the weavers of the town were noted for their skill in mechanics and the weaving of fine damask. Most of the inhabitants of Dunfermline were employed in the weaving industry and my Grandfather's father was an engineer and was accidentally killed in the factory. My Grandfather Robert was born in 1815, and naturally when he was old enough, entered the factory. In 1840, he married Elizabeth Struthers, daughter of John Struthers of the County of Dunfermline. He was then 25 years of age.

➤ Elizabeth occasionally would tell a story about Andrew Carnegie, the great steel magnate, as a boy. Both Robert and Elizabeth were children of fathers who worked in factories in Scotland. Every morning about nine o'clock, breakfast would be brought to the workers in the factory by their children. Andrew Carnegie's father was employed in the same factory as Elizabeth's father. At the time, Andrew was a healthy, barefooted factory man's son, who brought his father's breakfast to him in a tin pail. Elizabeth usually had some toast. "Young Carnegie was awful' fond o'toast and I gied him a wee bit o'it every morning."

➤ When the flourishing weaving industry was struck by a depression, many, including the Moodie family: Robert, his wife Elizabeth and their five children, Margret, David, William, Robert and Helen, set sail for Canada. James, John and Elizabeth were born later in Canada. During the voyage across in 1850, a child Dougal (Douglas) Munroe Moodie, (D. Aubrey Moodie's father) was born. Dougal was named after Dougal Munroe, the captain of the ship. The family landed in Montreal and made their way to Bytown, by boat. They traveled from Bytown to Manotick by shanty jumper as the bob sleigh was called. The roads were just trails in the bush.

➤ Bytown was at this time only a good-sized village. The Rideau Canal was a very important artery of commerce and travel at that time, and was the means of this section of the country being rapidly developed. So that naturally, my Grandfather Robert decided to take up land in this vicinity, and as he had two bothers who had settled near Manotick, David and Alexander, he naturally went there.

➤ My father, David, said during the first winter they spent here about all they had to eat was peas from which they made porridge, flour and even coffee. They also had a cow, but there came a time through the winter when the peas gave out. When they were in a desperate situation, he and my Grandfather drove the cow all the way from Manotick to Bytown in the middle of the winter to sell it to buy grain and other necessities. My father said, that while waiting for the sale of the cow, he almost collapsed from hunger and fatigue.

Dougal Munroe Moodie,
D. Aubrey Moodie's father

➤ During the first winter, they suffered intensely from the cold as the cabin hastily thrown together on their arrival at Manotick was not built to withstand the severe cold weather of the Canadian climate, and my father said that much of the time, he awakened in the morning with his bed covered with snow, and the temperature the same inside the cabin as outside.

➤ During the first summer, Robert worked for $10 per month to support the family of eight. Eventually, he would buy a bush farm near Twin Elm, fronting on the Jock River where they lived for seven years. They moved to Bells Corners in 1861 where Robert became involved in the hotel business and lived at a farm, (situated on the northwest corner of present day Moodie Drive and Robertson Road), until the last few years of their lives.

➤ Bells Corners at this time was a flourishing village and rivaled Richmond which considered their village of more importance than Bytown and some of the inhabitants even talked of Richmond becoming the capital of Canada. The traffic between Richmond, Bells Corners and Bytown became very extensive at this time and there were lively times around the Corners. I remember my dear mother speaking of the early days of fairs, and balls and social doings of the times. The village had a fairgrounds, horse racing was very popular, with many balls being held in the fairgrounds building which were the social events in this section. (The Carleton County Fair was held in Bells Corners until it was moved to Richmond, Ontario in 1894.)

➤ During this time, my Grandfather acquired the property for the building of a macadamized road between Bells Corners and Richmond and known as Corduroy Road (Robert's method of using deep fill to fill the soft muck of 1,000 yards of swamp succeeded where others before him failed. Brush was cut and laid across the road before it was covered with gravel.)

➤ A macadamized road was also built between Bells Corners and Bytown. A stage line was put in service between Richmond and Ottawa and continued in service up to a few years ago. (Later, the stage line was replaced with a seven-passenger car, operated by Harold Moore who owned the general store in Richmond and Herb Stinson who farmed.)

Bells Corners was a flourishing village and rivaled Richmond which considered their village of more importance than Bytown. Some even talked of Richmond becoming the capital of Canada.

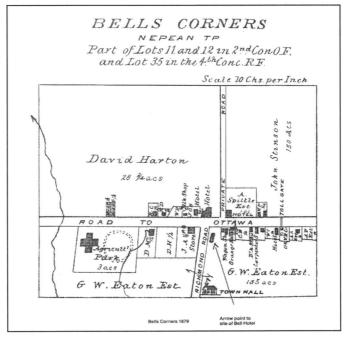

Map depicting Bells Corners in the year 1879

Robert Moodie's business acumen focused on the great potential of the sewing machine in pioneer households. He introduced the famous Gardner model to the county. (Carleton Saga)

A newspaper clipping celebrating Mr. and Mrs. Robert Moodie's 67 years of married life, notes that they were "both hale and hearty: Mrs. Moodie at 92 and Mr. Moodie at 90. To regularity in habits and temperate living, the aged couple attributed their present vigour and good health. Invariably, husband and wife retire to bed before half-past nine and get up early in the morning. Mr. Moodie has never smoked or used stimulating liquors, and today, can read the finest print without the aid of glasses, and can go into the field and take a turn with the men at work yet. Mrs. Moodie has a remarkably good memory and can sing by hour the songs of Auld Scotia, and if a good Scottish reel is struck up, can dance a measure yet."

A newspaper clipping (circa 1906): Mr. and Mrs. Robert Moodie, Aubrey Moodie's grandparents

Robert and Elizabeth Moodie experienced many milestones starting with their journey across the ocean, in supporting and raising their family in a new country, in surviving the Great Fire of 1870 that swept through Bells Corners, and in witnessing the birth of the railway and the advent of the car.

Robert Moodie died in 1911 at the age of 95. His wife, Elizabeth (nee Struthers), died in 1906 at 93. They are buried in the Bells Corners United Church Cemetery which is now shared with Bells Corners Anglican Church. At the time, they were survived by three daughters: Mrs. Alex (Margret) Spittal, Mrs. Richard (Helen) Shore of Hartney, Man., and Mrs. George (Elizabeth) Sparks, and four sons, John and Robert of Ottawa, William of North Gower and my father, Douglas (Dougal) of Bells Corners. They were predeceased by two children: James and David, a Bells Corners blacksmith, was killed when a stone wall collapsed during a high wind storm. Robert and Elizabeth had 42 grandchildren and 19 great-grandchildren.

The Early Years

1908 to 1932

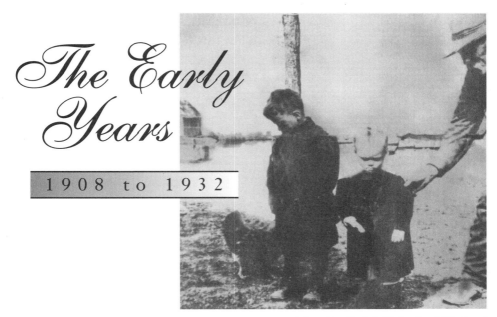

Aubrey Moodie, left, his brother Clifford and
their father Dougal Moodie

I was born on July 22, 1908 on the 100-acre family farm in Bells Corners in Nepean Township to Douglas Robert (Dougal) Munroe Moodie and Sarah Cummings. Years later, the farm was redeveloped as a shopping centre at the corner of Moodie Drive and Robertson Road.

I was baptized in 1908 at Drummond Presbyterian Church which became Bells Corners United Church. This was a large, active congregation consisting of rural families who would travel great distances to attend the service. Members were generous in their financial support of the church. Some of the families were the Armstrongs from Eagleson Road, the Griersons from Hazeldean, the Bouchers, Craigs and Stinsons from Corkstown Road, the Condies, Henrys, and Plunketts from Greenbank Road and the Robertsons from Bells Corners. The original church on Robertson Road houses a spa today.

My parents lived close to the church so we volunteered to be the caretakers. That meant starting the fire in the woodstove in the church basement on Saturday night to heat the Church in time for the service on

Sunday morning. It took some time to warm the sanctuary and rid the stone walls of frost because the building was not heated during the week. That church on Robertson Road is now used to house a spa.

People who came to the service were very well-dressed, some wearing coats of beaver or raccoon. They arrived by foot and if they traveled by horse and cutter, they were cloaked in buffalo robes to keep them warm. The sounds of the horses arriving and the bells on the harness ringing were magical. It was a great opportunity to see your neighbours and exchange family news.

I am told that in my earlier years, I often sat on Reverend Robert Gamble's knee for part of the service, much to the pleasure of the congregation. Reverend Gamble served from 1914 to 1918. Reverend J. McFarlane served from 1918 to 1925.

Going to church has been a major part of my life for more than 90 years. From 1934 to 1969, I served as a church elder with the Bells Corners Presbyterian Church and subsequently as a result of the church union, as elder at the Bells Corners United Church.

I grew up with my younger brother Clifford and our adopted sister, Annie McKee, who came from Scotland to live with us when I was eight or nine years of age. Annie was like one of our own. Later she married William Davidson and had a son Douglas and a daughter, Marilyn. Douglas became a professional engineer and married Marilyn Arnold. They live in Belleville. Douglas has two children: Lynn and Rob. Annie's daughter, Marilyn, became a legal secretary and made her home in Manotick with her husband Bruce Wanamaker. Clifford married Laura Greer. They had three children: Shelby, Lorraine and the late Greer.

My father, Douglas, was a sturdy Carleton County pioneer who loved to hunt and to fish. He spent his life farming the old-fashioned way. He milked cows by hand and raised turkeys and chickens to sell at the market. Father grew grain – mainly oats – and sold it to the owners of livery stables and to the proprietors of dairies and bakeries as feed for the horses used to deliver their products. He was a shareholder in the local Producers Dairy.

My father was a hard worker in his younger days and he did a bit of wrestling on the side. He frequented local fairs where he wouldn't mind challenging another man to a match. I think my sense of determination comes from my father.

I grew up with my younger brother Clifford (left) and our adopted sister, Annie McKee (right, with husband William Davidson).

I am a great believer in discussing problems with people. However, if I thought I was right, after I took the time to discuss problems with others, I didn't let go easily. I am proud of that trait. I didn't take the easy way out. The one lesson I learned from my father was to respect the opinion of the other fellow, regardless of the outcome.

Dad enjoyed taking us to Shirley's Bay on the Ottawa River where we used to catch beautiful white fish. When we arrived, we would stable the horses in Howard Davidson's shed. One day, Dad was in his boat when he heard men shouting for help. He rowed over to them as quickly as he could and managed to save two men. The third, unfortunately, let go of the boat and drowned.

I was six when World War I broke out. I remember my mother Sarah, like so many others who worked as volunteers for the Red Cross, spending hours and hours knitting socks and mittens to send to the boys overseas. She was a hard-working woman who served her family and her community by supporting the causes of the Women's Institute, our Church and the Community Club in Bells Corners. It was called social work then.

Sarah Cummings came from a large family in Manotick. One of my favorite recollections is Christmas at the Cummings homestead. Uncle Bob would invite the entire family. We eagerly looked forward to the 12-mile ride by horse and sleigh. We would prepare for the trip by heating bricks, wrapping them up and placing them in the sleigh to keep our feet warm. It was great to get together with our uncles, aunts and cousins.

When we arrived, the elders would play cards, talk and have a few drinks. We would all enjoy a great meal of turkey. Turkey was something special because Christmas was the only time of the year we ate it. Christmas at the Cummings became a 20-year tradition!

I have very poignant memories of the first Armistice in 1918. One of our cousins, Russell Cummings was returning – safe and sound – from World War I. Russell was due to arrive by train at Union Station located at Rideau Street and Sussex Drive. We stabled our horse at Britannia and planned to take the streetcar, from there, to meet Russell. Enroute, we were hit by a model T Ford. No one was hurt, but we were very concerned about being late. As it happened, when we arrived at Union Station we found the station jammed with crowds. Fortunately for us, the train was running late! Emotions were riding high and the flow of tears was unbelievable. We were like everyone else – so overjoyed to have our relatives and friends returning.

I was with my father when he died at the age of 76 in 1926. He had peritonitis, an infection that is treatable today. His last words were, "I don't know how you are going to get along without me."

Naturally, I quit school immediately to help support our family. I was 18 and just three months into high school.

We were novices when it came to the financial aspects of farming and at the time, farm dealers were very experienced at selling their wares. We realized if we were to prosper, we needed a silo and some machinery. Money was an issue so we agreed to sign a note to mortgage the farm.

My brother Clifford did most of the day-to-day work on the dairy farm and I sold the cream and the produce. In 1929, I became a member of the Carleton Milk Producers – a relationship that spanned 52 years. For me, it was important to belong to the organization that influenced your livelihood and particularly this one which recommended milk pricing.

Buying on a note in the good times isn't much of a gamble, but it is a very different story when the note comes due and economy is weak. That was the case when the stock market crashed in 1929 and was followed by the greatest depression known to North America. Money dried up. Unemployment was rampant and there were bills to pay. Some prominent citizens of Nepean lost so much money that they committed suicide. We were in debt and like many other farmers in the 1930's we worked hard to make ends meet.

In the early 1930's, Premier George S. Henry initiated a program to improve the roads. It was a make-work project to employ hundreds of men on relief. Notwithstanding the employment efforts by Premier Henry, his Conservative Government was defeated by Mitchell F. Hepburn's Liberal Party in 1934. Locally, the work was concentrated on a site west of Robertson Road. The engineer, a Mr. Angel made up a poem to describe the difficulties facing the workers and their horses that often became mired in the muck.

'Twas a muskeg minus a bottom
A swamp of the blackest kind
That since the time of Noah
Has never been known to dry.

Those days will never be forgotten. They were bad times and you knew what it was like to have a dollar.

Those days will never be forgotten. They were bad times and you knew what it was like to have a dollar.

Milk prices dropped to 50 cents a hundredweight. Prime Minister R.B. Bennett, who served from 1930 to 1935, introduced legislation known as the Farm Creditors Act. The Act provided relief for farmers who created debt during the good times and couldn't repay it during the Great Depression. An adjudication board was set up to rule on applications submitted by farmers who wanted to have their mortgage obligations dismissed. Seldom was the person holding the mortgage compensated for his/her loss.

One of my uncles, James Cummings, had no family and no debt. He did, however, hold some farm mortgages. The fellow owing the mortgages applied to have his debt forgiven. The board approved the application without compensation and my uncle was left a poor man. Many others found themselves in a similar situation.

We were in debt at the time, but we decided not to take advantage of the Farm Creditors Act. Instead, we worked hard to make money. We separated the cream from the surplus milk and delivered it on the streets of Ottawa.

One customer, Mrs. Moxon, lived on Laurier Avenue and I had to climb three, long flights of stairs to deliver a half-pint of cream for 10 cents. You might ask yourself why I would climb those stairs for 10 cents. There was one very good reason. Quite frequently, she would recommend a new customer who would take a quart of cream. Mrs. Moxon was a valued customer. She was the wife of a tailor who took orders for suits throughout the County of Carleton and she was a relative of Clarence Wilson who had a five-piece band. Known as the Wilson Orchestra, it was a very popular group of musicians who played at lawn socials and barn dances including the opening of Cecile Faulkner's new barn in the Lynwood community.

One of my best customers was the Arcadia Grill on Bank Street. The proprietors often bought a couple of gallons of cream. Then one morning, I went around and saw a bankruptcy sign on the door. I was left holding an account of $200.

In those days, cream was unpasteurized, that is until the law changed in 1938 when the Ontario Health Act required pasteurization of cream and milk for human consumption. You couldn't sell or give away cream unless you had the facility to heat it to a specific temperature and cool it immediately after. We couldn't comply, so that ended our cream business.

We did just about everything. We picked potatoes for fifty cents a day; we delivered loose hay to the many livery stables; and we sold chickens and fresh produce at the Byward Market. We would re-sell eggs we purchased from our neighbours, the Stinsons and the Moores. My profit was five cents a dozen. If I came home from the market with $25, I considered it a good day.

Mother was very resourceful during the Great Depression. Every fall, she invited friends to participate in her annual euchre tournament consisting of three six-hand tables. Matt and Martin Kennedy and Holly Acres were among the regulars.

Aubrey's mother Sarah is shown with a group of friends in this photo taken in August 1952. Back row from left: Eddie Logan, Mr. Allen, Mabel Logan; front row from left: Sarah Moodie, Sharon Logan and Mrs. Allen.

Mother always served a tasty goose supper and beer in a keg. Each player would contribute $5 to $10 dollars. The prize was one goose per victorious match. We raised 50 to 60 geese in anticipation of this event, so you can imagine how many games were played. They played all night and well into daylight. By morning, they were tired and a little tipsy. You never saw anything funnier than 18 people trying to catch the geese they had won after drinking beer all night. Mother held the tournament for years and she always made enough to more than pay the taxes. Fortunately, we didn't have to pay provincial or federal sales tax or unemployment insurance then.

Those were really tough times and not just for farmers. My mother was one of the hardest-working women I ever knew. During the summer, my mother prepared baked goods and we would travel by horse and buggy to sell the baked goods to the cottagers along the waterfront on Woodroffe Avenue. Hy Besson, a cottager and a car dealer from Winchester, was a great customer.

When we ran out of money, Mother would kill a few chickens, put them into a handbag and hitch-hike into Ottawa. Among her regular customers were the owners of MacIntosh and Watts. She would sell them the chickens and, at the same time, convince them to donate prizes for the euchre parties held at the Community Club in Bells Corners.

My mother also made friends with the owners of M. Caplan Furriers on Bank Street. The Caplans were wealthy people who owned a large, luxurious car. Often they called on us to take us for a drive. Before they arrived, we would walk to the railroad nearby to pick a couple of three-quart pails of wild strawberries which we sold to them for 50 cents a pail.

One of the popular outings was the drive to the Hildebrands, a German couple who owned a grist mill located on a sideroad between Eagleson Road and Bells Corners. The Hildebrands grew great rhubarb close to the mill. Now, grain was ground in the grist mill and the waste grain attracted rats which bred quickly. I will never forget the day we went to pick the rhubarb and the rats came running out of the rhubarb. You can just imagine the scene! (Johnnie, one of the Hildebrand's sons, was a fishing buddy of mine in later years. He did custom work using a thrasher and steam engine.)

I remember transporting grist by horse and sleigh – 10 to 12 bags at a time – to the Hildebrands to be ground into meal for cattle and pigs. One day, the sleigh got stuck on the railroad track. The train was upon us. The horse pulled away and I jumped off just before the train struck the sleigh. I guess it wasn't so bad because the railroad company compensated me for the loss. It was money we needed.

During the 1930's, we added to our income by delivering sandstone for the Campbell Sandstone Company to downtown Ottawa. It was quite an undertaking because Campbell's quarry was located two miles west of Bells Corners (Highway 17 and Corkstown Road) in the west end.

We had one team of horses and because we needed two teams to haul the sandstone, we formed a partnership with our neighbour Bob Moore. We drew sandstone by the ton up Wellington Street to be used to construct the Confederation Building at Bank and Wellington Streets. I remember the long hill starting at Booth Street. We would change the teams midway because it was such a tough climb.

Over the years, thousands of tons of sandstone were transported for use in major buildings such as the re-construction of the Peace Tower on Parliament Hill – destroyed in the terrible fire of 1916, the Royal Canadian Mint, Christ Church Cathedral, and LaSalle Academy.

While Bob Moore owned horses, he didn't own a car. During prohibition years, I often drove him to a bar in Hull on Saturday. That reminds me of a story about Bob who was a very practical man. He was sitting on an old-fashioned, three-legged stool as he milked a cow when a salesman, peddling minerals, stopped in. The salesman extolled the virtues of his mineral product as a way to improve the health of Bob's cows in years to come. Bob looked at him and said, "Your product is of no use to me. I just have to go to Williams' General Store and buy a bag of bran to get results tomorrow morning!"

Mother offered board to some of the sandstone quarry workers. In the summer, the workers would sleep in the garage with the exception of two older Scots – the Jamieson brothers. They had a bedroom in the house. I would sit and talk with them for hours and enjoy a few of the chocolates they always had. They were special people.

Many of these workers were from Wales and Scotland. They were the reason why the team from Bells Corners, a little rural village, won the senior soccer championship for Canada. Gordon Williams, the goalie, was from Bells Corners. He and his brothers Russell and Trevor also played on the Bells Corners hockey team. They had a sister Jenny and another brother, Emrys who I will tell you about later.

Their father, Dick Williams, kept a store which would be situated today at the southeast corner of Robertson Road and Richmond Road in Bells

Corners. It was a combination grocery, gas and post office and the gathering place for the community. If anything happened the night before, that's where you heard about it the next day.

The site of the general store eventually became another type of a community hub and the home of Nepean Township's municipal offices from 1966 to 1988. The Bells Corners Post Office eventually was moved to Northside Road in the Lynwood area. In later years, Emyrs Williams was responsible for defeating a move to have Bells Corners renamed as Lynwood. There was a lot of pride in the history and the name Bells Corners. I worked behind the scenes with the late Hon. Dick Bell to help defeat the idea.

We used to change our skates at the Belfords' home. They ran the black-smith shop and had two boys who loved to play hockey at the outdoor rink which would be located where Bells Corners Public School stands today. I played a little hockey but was never a good skater. Instead, I thoroughly enjoyed coaching the Bells Corners Hockey Team for 15 years. One particular year, the season culminated in a really exciting playoff for the Ottawa Citizen's Ottawa and District Intermediate Shield. We lost to Maxville but it wasn't for a lack of effort.

At 18 years of age, I became secretary-treasurer of the Bells Corners Community Club. I was active in raising funds for community projects such as purchasing land for the club. The Bells Corners Community Club was located where the Bells Corners Public School stands today on Richmond Road. The Club served as the social focus of Bells Corners drawing friends and neighbours – regardless of religion – together for card games, raffles and dances.

The Bells Corners Community Club was similar to today's community centres except that the onus was on the community to raise funds for cultural and recreational activities, not the municipal tax base. Everyone got involved and pitched in to help.

Skating and hockey were great pastimes for the children. Drawing water in barrels from the nearby creek to flood the skating rink was an arduous task, requiring horses and sleighs. There was obviously a better way to do this. A group of us, including John Dawson, worked well into the night to dig a well to supply the water.

Ella, D. Aubrey Moodie's wife, had four sisters and seven brothers. From top left are: Russell, Johnnie, Ella's father Bob Hand, Ernie and Tommy; bottom left are: Gordon, Lloyd and Vincent.

From top left are: Ruby, Aggie, Ella's mother Ida Hand nee Boucher, Jennie and Ella. Doris is in the centre.

We all got along. We did have some strained moments though when a local priest told his parishioners not to attend the Bells Corners Community Club. It was unfortunate because that action caused a rift in some families. Some chose to continue with the club. Others left.

Back in those days, the neighbours took turns to host house dances. There would be 20 or more people and we would dance to everything from the square dance to the fox trot and waltz. That's how I met my wife Ella in 1927. We were both 19. The fiddlers were playing and the caller bellowed, "Swing your partner." I was dancing with Ella and remember thinking, "She is a good dancer." Ella said later, that at the same time she was thinking, "He's the one!" She also had a boyfriend from Navan whom I met a couple of times at her home on Eagleson Road. Ella was the daughter of Robert Hand and Ida Boucher. They owned a 400-acre dairy farm which unfortunately, they lost when they fell upon hard times after the Great Depression. Ella's parents moved to Richmond where they lived for the rest of their days.

Before our marriage in 1933, my wife Ella worked as a housekeeper for $15 a month for Mrs. Meeks who was the wife of Charlie Meeks, the manager of Borden Dairy. Ella would do some baking which Mrs. Meeks would sell to help pay Ella's salary. The point is even well-to-do city folks were in need during the Great Depression.

Starting Out

Ella and I were married on June 3, 1933 in St. Matthew's Church on Bank Street by Reverend Hodder. His wife was the organist. Our families joined us in the celebrations as this wedding group photograph shows.

Ella Regina Hand and I were married on June 3, 1933 in St. Matthew's Anglican Church on Bank Street, near Lansdowne Park. Rev. Hodder officiated. We took a three-day honeymoon. When we left, we drove past the Hand homestead on Eagleson Road. Ella started to cry. She had already started to miss her family. The Hands were a very close-knit family. She had four sisters and seven brothers: Agnes, Jennie, Ruby, Doris, Johnnie, Ernest, Lloyd, Russell, Thomas, Vincent and Gordon. Ella, Ruby and Doris are living today.

Twin Elm became our home in 1936. We sold it to our son Doug in 1968 and moved in 1971 into our new home, just a few minutes away. (Ottawa City Archives)

After we were married, Ella and I lived with my mother and my brother Clifford and his wife Laura (nee Greer) at the farm in Bells Corners. My mother remained on the farm until her death on November 28, 1954. Edna was our first child. We didn't have a babysitter and we didn't have daycare and one of Ella's chores was to milk the cows. Ella would put Edna in a wicker basket and take Edna with her to the barn.

When Ella and I decided it was time to get our own place in 1936, I went to see Milton Cochrane at Almonte to ask him about renting a farm at Hazeldean. Milton was appointed by the Province of Ontario to manage the sale of property seized for non-payment of mortgage. Milton urged me to buy a farm for sale – and one in particular owned by Martin Kennedy at Twin Elm. He also warned me not to discuss the purchase with anyone in the community. We were Protestants moving into a Catholic community during a time when religion could become an issue, depending on how you conducted yourself.

When I contacted Tom Stinson to ask his advice about buying the farm, I didn't have a nickel to my name. Tom started out by saying he would lend me the money and then stopped short. "I'll do better than that," he said, "I will give you the money and if some day, you can pay me back, do it then."

We negotiated the deal without inspecting the 100-acre farm. I paid $4,000 for it, with $100 down and three percent interest on the balance. Mr.

Kennedy rented the inner part of the house from us for $7 a month. That $7 paid the salary of the hired man we needed to help us run the farm. Ella and I used the kitchen and the rest of the house.

Mr. Kennedy and his wife stayed with us for three or four years before they moved to Richmond. We enjoyed their company and played cards together on many nights. We were accepted by the neighbours, I think, in part, because we co-operated with Mr. Kennedy.

On May 1, 1936, I bought a team of horses at Leo Houlahan's auction sale and paid for it with a note. If you paid by a note, you needed a co-signer. Dan Cowick, one of my neighbours, backed me. In those days, people, especially farmers, had quite a bit of faith in each other. I planned to plant barley and purchased the seed from a well-known farmer, Gilbert Smith, at Goulbourn. I didn't have the money to pay for the seed, so I bought it on a promise to pay. Fortunately, grain prices for barley improved for the first time that year. Prices rose to 90 cents a bushel. In fact, there wasn't a better year to buy a farm. The note came due for the team of horses at the same time I received the cheque for the barley!

Twin Elm was home to our children from left: Judy, Donald, Sheila, Douglas and Edna.

We couldn't have been made more welcome nor had better neighbours at Twin Elm. When it came to the harvest and cropping, Scott Foster, Herb Stinson and others, were there to help. Those relationships continue today. When our farm buildings burned in 1960, we lost 27 head of cattle. We had many offers of help. Garnet Ralph came over to the house the next morning. He offered to cut the fence between our farms to allow us to drive our cows across his fields to access his milking equipment. We metered the milk and shipped it with Garnet's in the same milk tanker. Because of him, our milk cheque continued. We never lost our income.

Ella was born and raised in Nepean and she knew from the time she was a teenager what hard work was all about. Ella had no use for politics and I never brought my politics home. Nevertheless, she spent countless hours patiently waiting for me to conclude township discussions. However, she enjoyed the social aspects and accompanied me to many political functions.

When we moved to the farm at Twin Elm, our children were trained to work. Our sons Doug and Donnie would help on the farm by cleaning the stable and doing other chores. Doug stayed with farming. Donnie became a firefighter with the Nepean Fire Department. Our daughters are all close by. Sheila was manager of the Carleton Yacht and Golf Club and her husband, Ian McCurdie – now retired from the Ontario Provincial Police – live in Manotick; Judy is married to Donald Pratt, a former Ontario Government employee who now does consulting on assessment; and Edna is married to Harrison Thayer, now retired from the former Ottawa Hydro. Ella and I have 14 grandchildren and 18 great-grandchildren.

Twin Elm fronts on the Jock River. When we moved to Twin Elm, the river was clean enough for swimmers and a very popular spot for families.

Ella and I were returning home from Manotick one day, when we noticed cars lined up along the Jock River. When we stopped, we discovered a rescue attempt underway. Our daughter, Sheila, was in a boat on the Jock River with her first cousin Judy Boyd and a neighbour Leah Hammill, the daughter of Leo Hammill. They were trying to save a Montreal man from drowning.

The Hon. Richard. A (Dick) Bell presented my daughter Sheila, left, her cousin Judy Boyd (Lawlor) and her friend Leah Hammill (Cassidy) with the Canadian Humane Association's Honorary Testimonial Certificate for "heroic action and presence of mind in assisting in the rescue of Anthony McNeil, from drowning in the Jock River on August 27, 1958." (Photo by Newton)

He was a big man, making it difficult for them to pull him into the boat. They were able to float him back to the dock where they performed cardio-pulmonary resuscitation. Doctor Leach from Manotick was standing over them. "You're doing fine girls, keep it up," he said. They saved the man's life. Sheila had taken Royal Society Life Saving and St. John's Ambulance training – in Harry Leikin's barn, a program I had arranged as a member of the Agricultural Committee of the Kiwanis Club of Cityview.

These young ladies were honoured when the Hon. Richard A. (Dick) Bell, MP for Nepean-Carleton, presented them with a certificate from the Royal Canadian Humane Association at a Carleton Milk Producers' banquet at the Chateau Laurier in downtown Ottawa. We were so proud of Sheila and her friends. The point was, when Sheila was given the opportunity to use what she had learned, Sheila did her best.

The farm at Twin Elm was a full-time operation. Over the years, I was involved in many organized community activities including politics so I depended heavily on Ella to supervise the hired help. She was very good. At one point during the Second World War, we had a prisoner of war working for us. Every Sunday, he would polish the tractor as if he owned it. He was reluctant to return to Hamburg, Germany when the war ended in 1945.

Ella deserves a lot of credit for running the farm and keeping things organized at home. You need the support and understanding of your family to function in the political arena. I had that support and for that I am grateful.

Farming was obviously a big part of my life. I became a member of the Carleton Milk Producers when I was a teenager and was active for 50 years, up until 1979. It was an organization where you could learn from one another. Some of the skills I needed in later life were gained as a result of my earlier experiences showing prize cows at local school fairs and winning a public speaking contest.

One of my first actions was to recommend one price for milk regardless of where it was produced in Ontario.

Carleton Milk Producers was an excellent organization because it brought local dairy farmers together to share information about production and to make marketing recommendations to the Ontario Whole Milk Producers League (OWMPL) in Toronto. In the early days, we held meetings at the Court House on Nicholas Street.

Much later, I decided to run for election to the OWMPL. I was elected as second vice-president in a contest with George Blair and the next year, as first vice-president in a contest with Mr. Shouldice from Rocky Road in Quebec. The following year, I was elected president which automatically gave me a seat on the OWMPL's Board of Directors in Toronto.

The OWMPL represented all milk producers in Ontario and was responsible for milk pricing. At that time, the OWMPL had a policy of negotiating milk contracts with various distributors – a task I was asked to conduct on its behalf in this area. Several meetings were held with each distributor which made the commitment of time and effort substantial. I traveled miles and miles. One particularly blustery winter night after a meeting with the owner of the Eganville Dairy, I was forced to stop driving and to sleep at a farm because of the weather.

Coming to a common local agreement on milk pricing was commendable, however, there was more than one agreement in Ontario. That created price disparities between different areas of the province and between milk producers. One of my first actions, as an OWMPL board member, was to recommend one price for milk regardless of where it was produced in Ontario in order to stabilize the market. When I became second vice-president of the OWMPL, I pursued my views with vigor.

Wide-ranging discontent prompted the government to appoint a Royal Commission Inquiry into the Milk Industry in the 1960's. I worked with others to lobby for new legislation. We were successful because the government introduced the Milk Act in 1965 which established the Milk Commission of Ontario and the Ontario Milk Marketing Board (OMMB). The result was a comprehensive marketing plan which gave the OMMB the power to set milk quotas and prices for milk, establish pools, and buy and sell raw milk in Ontario.

We enjoyed a more personal way of doing business in those days. For example, Don Black, who was Ontario's agricultural representative, drove Bill Stewart Ontario's Minister of Agriculture, to my home to ask me to serve on the OMMB. At the time, I was a member of the Ontario Water Resources Commission (OWRC) and was concerned about serving both. Bill phoned Premier Bill Davis from my home to discuss the situation after I suggested that I would accept the Premier's decision. The Premier asked me to continue with the OWRC and to recommend a member for the OMMB. My choice was Alvin Stewart. Bill, Don and I went to Alvin's home. When we discovered he was at his cottage at Norway Bay that is where we went next. Alvin accepted the appointment and held the position for many years. His wife Joan served on the Ontario Apple Marketing Commission. They both thoroughly enjoyed their assignments.

BUCKINGHAM PALACE   PALAIS DE BUCKINGHAM

Mr. D. Aubrey Moodie and
Mrs. Ella Moodie

I am delighted to hear that you are celebrating the seventieth
anniversary of your wedding and send you my warmest
congratulations and good wishes on this splendid occasion.

Elizabeth R.

OTTAWA, 2003

Aubrey and Ella Moodie
6197 Perth Street
Richmond, Ontario
K0A 2Z0

Dear Aubrey and Ella,

It is a pleasure for me to send you my very best wishes on the
occasion of your seventieth wedding anniversary on June 3, 2003.
This is indeed a joyous event.

Marriage is a celebration of a very special bond, one that speaks
as much about friendship as it does about love. As you travel
through life together as a married couple, as partners and as
friends, your shared experiences and mutual respect are examples
to all those who share your journey.

I join your family and friends in wishing you continued happiness
in the years ahead.

Yours sincerely,

David Pratt, M.P.
Nepean-Carleton

Parliamentary Office
Confederation Building
Room 525
House of Commons
Ottawa, ON K1A 0A6

Hearty congratulations to both of you!

D. Aubrey and Ella Moodie

It is a great pleasure to send you best wishes
and warmest congratulations on the occasion of
your seventieth wedding anniversary

Jean Chrétien
Prime Minister of Canada
Ottawa 2003

Ottawa

Aubrey and Ella
Moodie

On behalf of Members of the City of Ottawa Council, it is a great
pleasure to extend to you my most sincere congratulations
on the occasion of your 70th Wedding Anniversary, June 3rd, 2003.
Best wishes for many more years of happiness.

Bob Chiarelli, Mayor

Grandma and Grandpa Moodie
On your Golden Wedding Anniversary
June 3, 1983

Not one of us remembers when our grandparents were wed
We asked our parents how it was and this is what they said—
At two p.m. on June the third in nineteen thirty-three
St. Matthews Church in Ottawa was just the place to be.
The handsome couple vowed that day to share each other's life
The Minister was Reverend Hodder – organist – his Wife.
We heard that on their honeymoon they really had a ball
But all they will admit is that they went to Montreal.
They bought a farm in Twin Elm where our parents went to school
In later years we'd visit there – we thought the farm was "cool."
We loved to go to Grandma's where we'd sing or play a game
She made us mitts and cookies to and loved us all the same.
Now Grandpa wasn't home too much except to sleep and eat
His active life in politics would find him on the street,
Each one of us was proud of him – and still we are today.
No matter what the issue was, our Aubrey'd have his say.
They left the farm eventually and built a lovely home
With just a bit of acreage for the two of them to roam.
Now Grandpa found it hard at first – was often bored and lost
But now he runs around all day and thinks he's still the boss,
Each fall they go to Florida and – gee we miss them so –
We sometimes go to visit though – away from ice and snow.
Last March our Grandpa went fishing in the ocean – what a scene
In April, back in Twin Elm, he was still a shade of green!
They bought a lovely cottage and it's up near Carleton Place
When Grandma talks about it, there's a smile upon her face.
It seems they have a motorboat which SOMEONE has to drive
She hopes he learns to master it and keeps them both alive.
For fifty years they've shared the fortunes that this life demands
We wish you both many more – together hand in hand.
Our heartfelt thanks to both of you from each and every one
You've made our lives much richer through your wisdom and your fun.
Please take this little bouquet as a symbol of our love
We ask each day – for both of you – God's Blessing from above.

Composed by Clara Baker, North Gower for the grandchildren

MOODIE FAMILY TREE

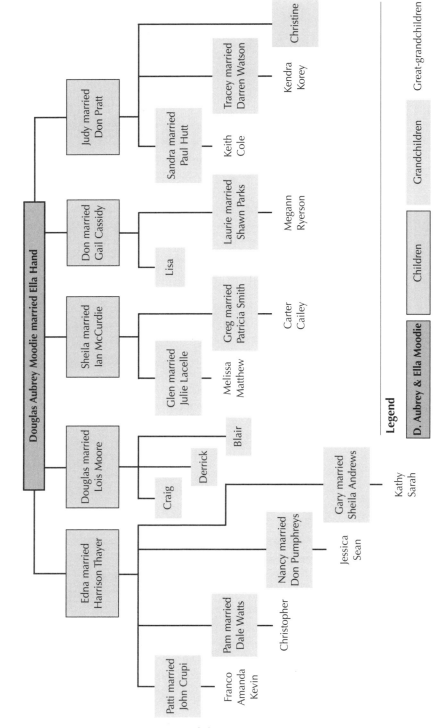

Douglas Aubrey Moodie married Ella Hand

Edna married Harrison Thayer

Douglas married Lois Moore

Sheila married Ian McCurdie

Don married Gail Cassidy

Judy married Don Pratt

Patti married John Crupi
- Franco
- Amanda
- Kevin

Pam married Dale Watts
- Christopher

Nancy married Don Pumphreys
- Jessica
- Sean

Gary married Sheila Andrews
- Kathy
- Sarah

Craig

Derrick

Blair

Glen married Julie Lacelle
- Melissa
- Matthew

Greg married Patricia Smith
- Carter
- Cailey

Lisa

Laurie married Shawn Parks
- Megann
- Ryerson

Sandra married Paul Hutt
- Keith
- Cole

Tracey married Darren Watson
- Kendra
- Korey

Christine

Legend

| D. Aubrey & Ella Moodie | Children | Grandchildren | Great-grandchildren |

Life-Long Learning

Aubrey and Ella admire the D. Aubrey Moodie Bursary Plaque. The bursary, awarded to the Carleton Board of Education secondary student (now the Ottawa-Carleton District School Board) achieving the highest marks, was announced at the testimonial dinner held in honour of Aubrey and Ella Moodie in 1970. Aubrey has made provisions to ensure the $200 bursary is awarded for a total of 60 years.

Although I left high school much earlier than I had planned, I have been involved in education, in one way or another, for much of my life. As a young man, my experience as secretary-treasurer, for School Section # 4 (SS #4) in Bells Corners and for SS #8 at Twin Elm where our children attended, provided me with some valuable lessons. At one point, I was secretary for both SS #4 and SS #8.

To give you some background, from the 1930's to the 1960's, local ratepayers were responsible for their school section (SS). A board of trustees was selected at an annual general meeting attended by residents living within the section. The board was responsible for the construction and the operation of its elementary school. Construction was financed by petitioning the township to authorize a bylaw to issue a debenture, the costs of which would be paid by the residents living within the school section, over a specific term as part of the education portion of their tax bill. As a funding partner, the Ministry of Education required the filing of many financial reports.

It was my job to keep the minutes of the meetings, purchase supplies, pay the bills and file reports with the Ministry of Education – for a nominal stipend of $15 a year.

I didn't have much schooling; consequently, I found it difficult to complete the Ministry reports. I sat up for hours at night doing the accounting because it had to balance to the penny. I persevered until it was done properly.

Aubrey attended the one-room schoolhouse known as SS # 4 in Bells Corners. Mrs. John Davidson taught 48 students. (Ottawa City Archives)

I was very reluctant to write my own letters over the years because of my lack of formal education. I was always concerned about incorrect spelling and poor grammar. I preferred to dictate my ideas to staff members and have them prepare the correspondence for me.

Evelyn Gigantes, a newspaper reporter at the time, asked me during one of my municipal election campaigns how I could possibly manage the operation of a municipality when I had a limited education. I told her I intended to use common sense. That response generated loud applause from the audience. Evelyn later became Minister of Community and Social Services when the New Democratic Party formed the Government of Ontario.

The world was changing in the postwar years after 1945. School facilities needed to expand to accommodate a burgeoning student population even before the impact of the postwar baby boom.

Evelyn Gigantes, a newspaper reporter at the time, asked me during one of my municipal election campaigns how I could possibly manage the operation of a municipality when I had a limited education. I told her I intended to use common sense. That response generated loud applause from the audience.

In 1948, Nepean's urban students attended Nepean High School on Broadview Avenue. Students in the remaining four rural school sections – Fallowfield, Jockvale, Twin Elm and McCullough – attended a continuation school in Richmond. There was a pressing need to build at least one more high school to serve the rural areas. That prompted Carleton County Council to form the South Carleton District High School Board (SCDHSB) in the late 1940's.

Carleton County Council consisted of the reeves and in some cases deputy-reeves of municipalities situated within the County of Carleton. The first order of business was to decide the location of a high school for students living in rural Nepean and the adjacent townships in Carleton County.

What a thorny debate it was. At that time, the majority of members of the SCDHSB and the Superintendent of Secondary Education wanted to build the new high school in Manotick. Edgar Gamble was the former Reeve of Richmond and the chair of the SCDHSB. His preference was a school in Manotick.

I had been appointed to the SCDHSB by Nepean Township Council, a position I relinquished when I was elected to township Council in 1950. As a member of Nepean Township Council, I also had a seat on Carleton County Council. A bylaw to authorize the debenture for the new high school went forward to Carleton County Council because it was to serve a number of municipalities within the county.

The bylaw contained a clause clearly spelling out the consequences: the Townships of Fitzroy, Huntley, Torbolton and March would join the Town of Arnprior if the high school in Manotick was approved. I was a keen supporter of Richmond as the preferred site. I knew I had to use a different type of logic to succeed.

I countered with a proposal to build two new high schools: one in Osgoode and the second in Richmond.

The high school speech was one of my first and most important speeches to Carleton County Council. It didn't make sense to me to see four municipalities break away from the County over this issue. Given that the rural area to be served by the new high school was too large for one school, I suggested two schools. The secondary school in Richmond would satisfy the four municipalities threatening to leave, and the secondary school in Osgoode would serve the community east of the Rideau River. That proposal changed the voting pattern and resulted in the opening of the high schools in Richmond and in Osgoode in 1952.

Looking back on the decision, I thought the construction of the new high school in Richmond would stimulate residential growth in this community and create a hub. The population boom didn't occur because the students were transported by bus to the high school and the teachers commuted from elsewhere.

In 1950, Nepean High School on Broadway Avenue was taken over by Ottawa's Collegiate Institute Board because the high school was located within the area annexed by the City of Ottawa. As part of the annexation agreement, we arranged to purchase education from Ottawa for Nepean's urban students attending Nepean High School. The Province of Ontario funded about 70% of the costs.

It didn't take too long to discover Ottawa wasn't the easiest to deal with financially. When the costs to purchase education became too high, we withdrew from the agreement and formed Nepean Township High School District Board in 1958. Bell High School and Merivale High School were opened in 1964, Confederation in 1967 and Sir Robert Borden in 1969.

Over the years, I could see that the system of individual school sections (SS) needed to be changed, so I started to promote the "township school area (TSA), an objective of the Ontario Government. Some citizens opposed the TSA because they feared a loss of control. Becoming part of a TSA meant the election of trustees using the formal municipal election process. It also meant sharing school board assessment with other schools located within the larger township school area, a prospect that caused consternation among some parents.

Reform began in 1952 when ratepayers supporting the individual public school sectors in the Bells Corners and Eagleson Road areas agreed to form the larger township school area (TSA # 1). A second TSA covered Cityview in 1958.

I recall a public meeting held by Nepean Council at Greenbank Public School – a one-room, stone schoolhouse – to discuss its inclusion in a TSA. The timing was good because some of the local assessment base had been lost because of expropriation of land by the Government of Canada. But not everyone agreed. The room was overflowing with citizens who came to express their views. Council passed the bylaw amalgamating the sections. Matt Henry was one of the vocal opponents to the plan. He never supported me politically again.

Now, we had quite a mix. In Nepean, there were TSAs which required the election of trustees using the formal municipal election process and a pooling of assessment and there were SSs where local residents chose their trustees using a less formal approach and enjoyed exclusive, albeit unbalanced, access to assessment.

In the early 1960's, I took steps to encourage the formation of one single township school board for Nepean Township. Consolidation of finances and facilities into a single school board, we believed, would result in larger grants and more specialized teaching in areas such as home economics, industrial arts and programs for those who were developmentally delayed. Common salaries, cost-savings from bulk purchasing and centralized administration were some of the other benefits. We were also faced with accommodating an increasing number of school-aged children. The discussion ignited public opposition and particularly from citizens in the Merivale area who didn't want to share the school taxes from the tank farms and the surrounding industrial area.

The population exploded from 16,500 in 1960 to more than 41,000 by the mid 1960's and reached approximately 60,000 by the end of the decade.

I received a telephone call from Erskine Johnston, the local MPP at the time. He advised me that the Province of Ontario planned to consolidate schools under one board in Nepean and similarly across the province, so we waited. During that period, we experienced phenomenal population growth and a housing boom. The population exploded from 16,500 in 1960 to more than 41,000 by the mid 1960's and reached approximately 60,000 by the end of the decade.

At one point, a worried Desi Fitzgerald came to see me about building a Catholic school in Bells Corners. Desi and I went to school together. Desi started off by saying that he was told not to approach me because I was a member of the Orange Lodge and therefore would never support the construction of a Catholic school. From my perspective, provincial legislation permitted the school to be built and that was all there was to it. I have always said that one of Nepean's great strengths was the fact that we have so many churches of different denominations that do such good work for the community.

Township public school areas, created by combining TSAs and SSs or by amalgamating SSs, came into being in the mid-1960's. The Province of Ontario established a county board of education for the public school system in the name of the Carleton Board of Education, and the six Catholic school boards in Nepean merged into the Carleton Roman Catholic Separate School Board. The first meeting of each Board was held on December 9, 1968. Ottawa residents were served by the Ottawa Board of Education and the Ottawa Roman Catholic Separate School Board. These milestones coincided with dissolution of Carleton County Council and the creation of its successor, the Regional Municipality of Ottawa-Carleton. The role of the City of Ottawa radically changed in that it not only contributed financially to region-wide initiatives; the political voice it lacked on Carleton County Council was now represented at Regional Government.

After I was defeated as Reeve of Nepean Township Council in the 1969 municipal election, my friends and colleagues held a dinner in honour of Ella and me. During the dinner on February 28, 1970, I was delighted to hear the proceeds from the evening would be donated to the Queensway-Carleton Hospital. We also announced a bursary would be established in my name. It is awarded annually to the Carleton Board of Education (now the Ottawa-Carleton District School Board) student attaining the highest marks. I made

In framing a budget, we give high priority to education. We taxpayers can be assured that this school is an investment for the future, the dividends from which will exceed any other we may have. One of the primary factors in the making of our civilization was our educational system, and from its primitive beginnings to this modern day, when we experience and observe the very acme of sophisticated achievement, it has been an onward and upward progress. What was once a rare privilege to the few now becomes the right and opportunity for all young people.

Aubrey Moodie at the 1972 Dedication of D. Aubrey Moodie Intermediate School

the necessary financial arrangements to ensure the $200 bursary would be awarded for 60 years. The money is not intended for educational purposes. It is "play money" to be used by the student to pursue leisure activities as a diversion from the long hours of study. The award is being administered on my behalf by the Bells Corners United Church.

I was honoured, again in 1970, when Carleton Board of Education Chair William Dakin proposed a new school, under construction on Moodie Drive, be named to recognize my contribution to education. Just a few weeks ago, I listened to a tape of the opening of D. Aubrey Moodie Intermediate School which brought back many memories.

My greatest personal challenge was to live up to my commitment to provide adequate educational facilities and good roads. I believe I did that. Towards the end of the 1960's, there were 18 public schools, nine Catholic schools and four secondary schools.

Thursday, June 5th, 2003

Mr. Douglas Aubrey Moodie
6197 Perth St.
Richmond, Ontario

Dear Mr. Moodie,

This year, I will be graduating from a school that is probably really important to you. Most of my enjoyed days have been at the wonderful school that has been named in your honour. I have learned many valuable lessons here, socially and academically over the past years. All of the teachers and students are welcoming and friendly, which is why my experiences at Douglas Aubrey Moodie Intermediate School have been so successful.

On Tuesday, June 24th, at 9:00 a.m. our school will be holding a grade eight graduation ceremony, and we would be privileged if you, the Father of Nepean, would be able to attend this special service. Our Language Arts class thinks that it would be great if you would be able to come and share this day with the graduates, since the school is named after you, and means a lot to you.

This is my third year living in Nepean, and I will be moving to Saudi Arabia at the end of July. I would like to thank you for all you have done for us, and your work is very much appreciated by the Nepean citizens. I am very grateful that you are taking your time to read this letter. Our class, as well as the rest of the school, would really appreciate it if you could come. We will understand if you are not able to attend, but your presence would mean a lot to the students and teachers at D. Aubrey Moodie School.

Sincerely,

Alia Jundi, 7/8H

Learning the Political Ropes

Nepean Township Council of 1950 consisted of from left: G.B. Acres, Len Davis, Aubrey Moodie, Reeve Tom Keenan and Hugh Davidson. (Ottawa City Archives)

The first time I sought a position on Nepean Township Council in 1948, I didn't make it. Here's what happened. Nepean Township Councillor Col. Ernie Denison and three others came up to the house on the farm to ask me to run as a rural candidate. I turned them down because I was already a member of the South Carleton District High School Board. About two weeks later, I changed my mind. Col. Denison was concerned that my decision came too late to get organized, but I decided to run anyway. Three councillors were to be elected. I ran fourth out of seven. That experience helped me to prepare myself for the future. Howard Henry, a Nepean councillor, approached me shortly after my defeat. "Do you have any idea who the next deputy-reeve will be?" he asked. I said, "No."

Not everyone was pleased with my decision to get involved in municipal politics. One of my relatives told me that I had disgraced the Moodie name and never spoke to me again.

Howard responded with, "Aubrey Moodie!" I believe the exposure I
received, even though I lost the first election, was part of the reason I was
acclaimed initially as Deputy-Reeve in 1949 to serve in 1950.

Looking back, 75 years ago it was difficult to be elected in Carleton
County unless you belonged to a fraternal organization such as the Free
Masons, the Orange Lodge or the Knights of Columbus. Being a member
of an organization served a very useful purpose because you learned everything from how to conduct a meeting to the importance of administration.
I have been a member of the Free Masons for 50 years and the Orange
Lodge, since I was 18 years of age. I have never let religion dictate
decisions. Very recently, I was honored by the Free Masons when I was
presented with a 50 year-pin. The Orange Lodge commemorated my
70-year membership with a plaque.

Not everyone was pleased with my decision to get involved in municipal
politics. One of my relatives told me that I had disgraced the Moodie name
and never spoke to me again.

Before I focus on some of the issues we faced, it is important to provide
some background on the political landscape. In 1948, Nepean Township
Council publicly supported the development of a federal district which
would include Nepean Township. The plan, dubbed the "Washington of
the North" was endorsed after Nepean Council traveled with the National
Planning Board to visit Washington, Philadelphia and New York. Nepean
Council saw this as an opportunity to improve local services at the Federal
Government's expense and to benefit from co-ordinated planning. Nepean
Reeve Harry Parslow was very supportive of the plan but somewhat
impatient about the proposed development and even more so with the
slow motion schedule, which called for the spending of perhaps $2 million
a year for the next 50 years. "Why not speed it up, and spend $4 million a
year for the next 25 years?" he was quoted as saying in a newspaper article.

But while Council was unanimous on the creation of a federal district,
Council was divided by the City of Ottawa's unexpected application in June
1948 to the Ontario Municipal Board to annex 13,000 acres in the
Township of Nepean.

Deputy-Reeve Frank Boyce expressed vehement opposition to the annexation of Nepean on the basis that it would lead to the disintegration of

Carleton County. Councillor Boyce was an employee of the Federal Government who placed labourers in the farming community so he was quite familiar with rural concerns. Reeve Parslow saw the annexation as part of natural progression, one that would benefit citizens. He really believed that the Township had no future. Councillor Howard Henry thought the voters should decide.

From my perspective, rural voters were very conscious of expenses and they had a desire to keep the Township of Nepean alive. Most of them were quite knowledgeable about Nepean's history and supported the policies of Carleton County Council.

Municipal voters were divided over annexation when they went to the polls in 1948. The rural community, which was not in favour of annexation, prevailed when Tom Keenan, a farmer from the Merivale area, defeated Reeve Parslow. However, some members of Council, who supported annexation, won their seats.

Now, there were two new heads of Council: Reeve Thomas Keenan in Nepean and Ottawa Mayor E.A. Bourque who defeated George Nelms.

Shortly after the election, the Ontario Municipal Board (OMB) issued the order allowing Ottawa to annex 13,000 acres in Nepean, effective January 1, 1949 – taking in all of urban Nepean and 6,000 acres of farmland. That encompassed all of the lands south of the Ottawa River, bounded by Britannia Village, south to the CNR line, east to Woodroffe Avenue, south beyond Slack Road and west to the Rideau River.

Carleton County Council applied, unsuccessfully, to the Ontario Supreme Court to appeal the OMB's ruling because it was going to lose approximately 35% of its assessment to the City of Ottawa.

However, as a result of skilful negotiations initiated by Reeve Keenan with Mayor Bourque, a new annexation plan emerged: the acreage to be annexed was reduced to 7,420 acres, effective one year later on January 1, 1950.

This conclusion was the result of some solid work by Reeve Keenan. While Nepean's downtown and the township hall in Westboro were now situated inside the new City of Ottawa boundaries, the lands located south of Baseline Road and west of Fisher Avenue would remain in Nepean.

In my opinion, Reeve Keenan never received the credit he deserved. If Henry Parslow had been elected in 1949, Nepean would not have survived because Reeve Parslow favoured joining the City of Ottawa. What Tom did, in successfully negotiating a greatly reduced annexation, was a major accomplishment. Tom needed some appreciation from the citizens of Nepean for what he had done.

Even though, Tom had accomplished a great deed, Tom believed the Provincial Government and the City of Ottawa had taken advantage of Nepean through the annexation. He was convinced his political affiliations as a Liberal interfered in the negotiations with the Conservative Province of Ontario.

Consequently, he took very little interest in the division of assets and liabilities in the years to follow. We had a difference of opinion on the division, but it was all on a friendly basis. Often, I would meet him for lunch at his farm. His father, Dave, used to enjoy the many conversations we had.

The division of assets and liabilities was very difficult. Legislation stipulated that the township hall remain with the municipality being annexed. In the negotiations, Ottawa took the position that it should be valued and included in the division of assets. You can imagine the arguments over that. We owned the building and believed we should be paid for it.

An arrangement was made for City of Ottawa and Township of Nepean staff to share space at the Township Hall in Westboro until Nepean built a new one. Ottawa staff occupied the ground floor and Nepean staff used the second floor. Emotions were running high between the two employee groups. When the disagreements

Nepean's downtown and its Township Hall in Westboro were now located in the City of Ottawa as a result of the City of Ottawa's annexation of 7,420 acres of land effective 1950.

reached a zenith, Nepean Township Clerk-Treasurer Andy McLean locked out City of Ottawa staff from the Township Hall, a move that produced newspaper headlines across Ontario. Andy must have been acting on the orders of the Reeve. As tensions waned, meetings were held and the difficulties were resolved.

There were some strong feelings associated with the Township Hall because of its long history. It was constructed in 1896 under the direction of Reeve G. Boyce and renovated in 1942. The interior was destroyed by fire on March 22, 1943. The township hall was rebuilt and used until November 12, 1966 when the new township hall in Bells Corners was opened by the Hon. Wilf Spooner, Ontario Minister of Municipal Affairs. Just as an aside, the Minister flew into the Carp Airport where he was met by Erskine Johnson, MPP who was to take him to the opening. It was a bitterly cold evening, so the pilot left the heater running. Technical difficulties were experienced which prevented them from flying out, as planned. There was one very irate Minister.

Municipal elections were held every year during the 1940's and up until 1955 when they began to be held every two years. After the annexation, money was scarce and we had yet another election ahead of us. There were three councillor positions and four candidates nominated. Everybody was concerned about the expenses to run the election so the four agreed to put their names in a hat and draw. The person whose name was drawn would withdraw his nomination. Gordon Greer's name was drawn, he withdrew, and the cost of an election was saved. That is how we managed difficult situations.

We also had long memories about voters' reactions to spending money. In the 1930's, Reeve G. Herbert Bradley, a well-known farmer from Merivale, refused to raise taxes. He was defeated by Robert Mackie who did raise taxes because the municipality was on the verge of bankruptcy. Now the voters didn't appreciate Reeve Mackie's action even though it actually saved the Township. He was defeated in the next election after serving just one year as Reeve.

I was acclaimed as Deputy-Reeve for Nepean Township for 1950, 1951, 1952 and 1953. At the time, Nepean Township Council members were paid $10 a meeting and Carleton County Council members received $7 per meeting. The County Clerk kept an attendance sheet and at the end of the meeting, each member signed it and was paid in cash. Once the Warden reviewed the attendance sheet and signed it, the Clerk was authorized to go to the bank to arrange for the next draw. By way of comparison today, Ottawa's City Councillors earn $56,000 and the Mayor receives $110,000 annually. Part of the salary is tax deductible and all members are eligible for a pension – a benefit that came into being after Regional Government was formed in 1969.

The post annexation years were difficult. Planning and approval processes were tangled up in jurisdictional and representational issues as well as the bad blood generated by the annexation. What was the purpose of the annexation? Was it to advance the creation of a federal district as part of the National Capital Plan or was it a successful land development acquisition by the City of Ottawa?

Look at the players. We had: the Federal District Commission (FDC) – the predecessor to today's National Capital Commission (NCC) – which was responsible for the implementation of the Gréber Report.

We had provincial legislation that gave local planning authority powers to the Ottawa Planning Area Board (OPAB) which affected Nepean, but there was no specific provision for Nepean representation on the OPAB until 1955. The OPAB supported the FDC's vision for development. But local councils approved subdivisions and enacted zoning by-laws. I will deal with this issue in greater detail in Chapter Seven: Protecting the Rights of Property Owners.

Our resources were stretched to the limit after the annexation, another point of contention. Tom Keenan and I had very different approaches to solving problems. For example, a heavy snowfall often took two to three days to clear up. Tom's response to citizens who complained was to tell them to wait. I would go to the Road Superintendent, Bob Neil, to discuss the problem. The truth was we just didn't have the equipment. When you explained the situation to citizens, they understood. They would accept things then where today they wouldn't. I was always able to maintain good public relations with our citizens and I knew the value of a Council that worked together.

Taking the Reins

In 1955, one year after my election as Reeve for the Township of Nepean, I was selected by my peers as Warden for Carleton County Council (CCC). It would be the first of three terms as Warden – 1955, 1962 and 1966.

D. Aubrey Moodie, Warden
(Ottawa City Archives)

Tom Keenan, Warden
(Ottawa City Archives)

When Reeve Tom Keenan decided to retire in 1954, I let my name stand with Tom's full support. I was elected and served as Reeve of Nepean Township Council for the next 15 years until my defeat in 1969 to Andrew S. Haydon. Nepean residents were either pretty shrewd farmers who followed politics or new residents who moved to Nepean because of the low taxes. Both the Township of Nepean and Carleton County Council held the same view: hold the line on taxes. Any increases were linked solely to growth.

As Reeve, I automatically had a seat on Carleton County Council – the predecessor to the Regional Municipality of Ottawa-Carleton. As a member of two levels of municipal government, you made local decisions affecting the Township of Nepean and decisions on broader county-wide issues.

Township Councils were responsible for matters such as police, fire, recreation, local roads, bylaws, planning, and tax collection on behalf of the township, the County and local school boards. Carleton County Council was responsible for matters such as health, homes for the aged, the operation of the County Court House, jail and appointment of juries, major roads through the Ottawa Suburban Roads Commission, and some educational issues and eventually the Ottawa Planning Area Board.

When I decided to run for Reeve in 1954, my opponent was Benny Acres, another sitting member and a good councillor. His father, Holly, sat as the local MPP for 30 years. There were two issues. Most of the voters lived in the urban area of Nepean. I was from the rural area. My opponent tried to make an issue over the fact that citizens would have to pay long distance telephone charges to call me at home. I responded that he was a cattle drover who was often out of town. "Which would you prefer?" I asked. "Someone you can't reach most of the time or someone you can reach with a ten cent phone charge and get results?"

The second election issue focused on the development of a road we know today as Moodie Drive. The only way you could drive it in the winter was with a team of horses. Benny insisted that developing the road was a waste of money. I approached it from the point of view that Ontario would pay 100% of the cost because it was a development road in a rural municipality. I was elected, and within two years, we had it built and paid for by the Province of Ontario at no cost to the municipality.

That wasn't good enough for me. It was quite a popular road, although some said it was overbuilt. One year after it was built and while attending the Ontario Good Roads Convention, I visited several hospitality suites to invite contractors to locate to Nepean.

One of the companies I approached was Ontario Brick. I was told if I could locate a property on a paved road so the brick wouldn't break as it was transported, a sand pit to make the brick, and access to water, company officials would be most interested in re-locating. When I returned home, I acted as a go-between to arrange for an option on a suitable parcel of land from Dr. Stevenson. Shortly after, Ontario Brick made its decision to build the plant on the site. Ontario Brick company president Bruce Wheeler attended a Council meeting to request the name of the road be changed from a concession road to Moodie Drive. I absented myself from the discussion by vacating the Chair. When I returned, Councillor Grant Carman advised me that Council approved the renaming to Moodie Drive.

There was a lot to be done in the 1950's. Not one of the 50 miles of major roads in the township was paved. We had no recreational facilities. We didn't have a police department and we didn't have a fire department. There were no sewers and no water distribution system and we had one employee, Leo Driscoll who was a truck driver at that point.

I had a technique I used when we were approaching or being approached by companies to locate in Nepean. I would try to find out where they did their banking and, once I knew, I would ask that bank manager to help me research the company. You have to have the facts.

As Nepean expanded, it became an attractive location for many businesses, but we had to work for them. Bells Corners was becoming attractive because of the availability of land and its access to the highway and railway. Before Computing Devices came to Bells Corners in 1956, one of its requirements was to have access to a sophisticated telephone service, more than what was offered by the local Hazeldean Telephone Company. At the time, I was managing-director of the telephone company. We were a little company that grew over 25 years from a switchboard with two operators to a 24-hour service with eight operators. Nonetheless, I held the view that it was time to sell the company to Bell Canada because we couldn't handle Computing Devices' requirements and I didn't want to lose the company to another municipality. John Davis of Fallowfield opposed the sale, but it went ahead.

The pace was hectic, but there were no caustic, continuous public confrontations with Ontario, the Federal Government or the National Capital Commission. We worked together to try to resolve the issues and between securing government grants and creating lot levies rather than depending solely on property taxes or borrowing through debentures, we managed our finances responsibly.

I was very involved in the Progressive Conservative Party and maintained regular contact with the Ministers in the Ontario Government. Whenever I went to Toronto, I made it a point to go to the coffee shop at the Royal York Hotel in the morning because that's where many of the Ministers had breakfast. I met with the Hon. George Dunbar – a native of Richmond, the Hon. Lorne Henderson, the Hon. Bill Stewart, the Hon. Frank Miller, John Root of the Ontario Water Resources Commission and many others.

Not everyone had the same style. During one election campaign in which George Dunbar was seeking election, he was heckled by a man at the back of the room. George stood up and said, "I know your history. I also know your taxes are in arrears so you better shut up."

Nor did everyone want to work together to find solutions. I was Warden of Carleton County Council in 1955, 1962 and 1966. Agriculture, then and now, contributes substantially to the local economy and as a result, I have always been a supporter of agricultural fairs. As Warden for Carleton County Council, I was a member of the Board of Directors for the Central Canada Exhibition (CCE). There was a move to relocate the Central Canada Exhibition from Lansdowne Park to a new home.

I knew of land for sale which was close to the highway and waterfront. It was the old Ottawa Electric Railway property which eventually was developed by Minto as Bayshore. Not everyone appreciated my view. One of the members of Ottawa's Board of Control, a Mr. Pingle said later, "If

Carleton County Council for 1951: Top row from left: A.E. Davidson, J.C. Donnelly, J.B. Potvin, Warden Dr. E. F. Johnston, L. Cantin, T.A. Dolan, and D.A Moodie; middle row from left: D.B. Cruikshank, H. Spearman, V.E. Major and J.E. Gamble; bottom from left: J. Boland, W.R. Wilson, T.C. Keenan, County Treasurer H.E Coldrey, C.R. Riddell, H. Craig and M. Robert. (Ottawa City Archives)

Aubrey Moodie thinks Ottawa is going to move its exhibition out to Nepean, he has another thought coming." Interestingly, the relocation of this exhibition has yet to happen 48 years later.

It is always important to collaborate on issues if you plan to succeed. Gloucester Reeve Earl Armstrong and I had that type of relationship. We had many discussions, but at no time, would we ever let it be known that we were in disagreement and at all times, we kept it fair. That was particularly important because we both sat on Carleton County Council. In previous years, before I became a member, the rural municipalities would work hard to pit Nepean and Gloucester against one another. Nepean and Gloucester each had four votes. Other county politicians figured that as long as Nepean and Gloucester disagreed with one another, they would cancel out each other's votes by voting against each other. That would destroy the voting block Nepean and Gloucester had when the politicians worked together.

The Gloucester Reeve and I co-operated on many issues including the creation of the health unit which I will cover later and the police force. At one point, we were involved in negotiations with our joint police force. Our original force had been absorbed into Ottawa as part of the annexation in 1950.

When the OPP withdrew its police service, the Gloucester-Nepean Police Force was formed in 1958. Magistrate Harry Williams and Judge Honeywell, Earl Armstrong and I were negotiating with the Police Committee and we couldn't reach an agreement. Rather than let it go to arbitration, I suggested that we all go over to the Albion Hotel.

The police negotiators couldn't believe we would be seen in a hotel with them. They really appreciated the gesture. At our next meeting, we had an agreement.

Looking back, I may have been a little too determined. On another occasion when we were negotiating a contract for the Gloucester-Nepean Police Force, discussions weren't progressing well so I said to one negotiator, "If you don't watch yourself, you will be out of a job." The union representative retorted with, "You can't say that." "Wait and see," I said.

Both Earl and I were in favour of having our own police department which prompted me to recommend the dissolution of the joint police force. I told

Gus Wersch was hired as Sergeant when Nepean Township Police was formed on January 1, 1964. He was to become Chief of Police.

the group, "We are going to be fair. We have hired a chief and a sergeant. Anyone who wants to apply, can." I don't think it was unfair, because people accepted it. Our policy was to employ as many of the former police officers who applied as we could. Only one officer chose to go to Gloucester.

Nepean Police Department came into being on January 1, 1964. John Rankin was the first Chief of Police. E.G. (Gus) Wersch, an experienced Ontario Provincial Police Officer, was appointed Sergeant. Gus Wersch became the Chief later. Nepean Police Services became part of a regional police service on January 1, 1995.

Roads were such an important part of our infrastructure.

In the 1950's, Woodroffe Avenue was just a narrow gravel road. Now, John Dawson, A.J. Fitzsimmons and Harold Kidd were war veterans and pretty good buddies on the Ottawa Suburban Roads Commission (OSRC). They wanted funding to upgrade 10 miles of rural roads – from Richmond to Stittsville. The upgrading would result in a reclassification from county road status to suburban road status and assumption by the OSRC. They asked Carleton County to support the plan and the transfer of the roads to the OSRC. Approval for funding to upgrade the road was required from the Province of Ontario.

I was hoping to convince the OSRC to take ownership of Woodroffe Avenue, south of Baseline Road. If the OSRB assumed it, Woodroffe would be upgraded. My proposal was in jeopardy because of the Richmond to Stittsville proposal, so I countered with another proposal at Carleton County Council. We should approach the Minister of Highways with a request for funding to connect the road from Kemptville to Fitzroy and build a bridge to Quyon. Goulbourn Reeve Dr. Harold Spearman thought it was a good idea and as did the rest of Carleton County Council so a motion was sent to the Minister. I was bluffing. I wouldn't be unhappy if the Ministry approved it. But my preference was the Woodroffe upgrade. I didn't think the Minister would approve my counterproposal and he didn't. That left the Woodroffe proposal on the table. The decision was to upgrade Woodroffe to 100' wide and have it assumed by the OSRC. Later, when a plan of subdivision, for property west of Woodroffe and north of Baseline, came up for approval at the Ottawa Planning Area Board, there was no provision for a continuation of the widening. I insisted on it and the motion was carried to widen Woodroffe to the Queensway.

Once Woodroffe Avenue was approved, Alonzo Craig and Alvin Stewart registered a subdivision that included a 66-foot road – Meadowlands Drive, between Woodroffe Avenue and Merivale Road. They also registered a park without a name. That park came to be known as Nameless Park for years after. I believed Meadowlands should be a through street and therefore wider so, I strongly opposed it when it eventually came forward.

Don Jeffrey, Nepean's Deputy-Reeve at the time, supported the developers. I was so determined not to be swayed that I suggested I would resign if he would do the same and we would let the public decide who was right in a vote. I later came to the conclusion that my offer to resign was a bad decision on my part. It was fortunate Don did not accept the challenge.

I was convinced that the road needed to be widened to 86 feet, so I called Central Mortgage and Housing Corporation to request the mortgages be withheld. Soon after, Russell Boucher, Alonzo and Alvin came to my home on a Saturday morning to ask me to withdraw my objection. I refused and when they realized I was not going to change my mind, they accepted my position. Later, I went to Toronto to support them in their application for funding for the development. I think that it is fair to say they graciously accepted my opinion and our friendship continued.

I believe the suburban roads were managed very well. We had excellent staff including engineer Lee Shearer who later moved to Victoria.

In the early 1960's, as Chair of Carleton County's Roads Committee, I introduced a plan to standardize road widths and reconstruct and pave all of the county roads in Carleton. Once the plan was approved by Carleton County Council, we presented it to Ontario's Minister of Highways the Hon. Jim Allen. He approved the plan. The Ministry would finance 50% of the costs in advance of construction and the County and the City of Ottawa would finance the balance equally by debenture. Approximately 65 miles of road, including some Ottawa suburban roads, were standardized, reconstructed and paved. In fact, when Regional Government was formed in 1969, all county roads qualified as regional roads. We didn't have consultants. The engineering was completed by the County. Land required for road widening was purchased from landowners in return for fences.

Shortly after, we also received approval from the Minister to develop the Dwyer Hill Road, from Burritts Rapids to the boundary road near Arnprior. It was constructed by the Ontario Government at no cost to County Council or the OSRC.

County Council benefited because Ontario Government believed good roads leading into Ottawa were fundamental to the economic success of Ottawa. That is why the funding formula was based on a 50% contribution from Ontario and 25% each from the City of Ottawa and Carleton County Council.

As a member of Carleton County Council, I had a few embarrassing moments such as the day local police raided the social room we had set up at the County Court House. Just moments before, Tom Keenan and I had left the building. The social room was in the caretaker's apartment which was located within the Court House. It was a place to go, before or after a meeting, to talk about business or just relax. Carleton County Council members chipped in money to pay for refreshments. At the time, I was drinking ginger ale.

This was all perfectly legal, or so we thought, until one day a newspaper reporter called the police to tell them the social room should be raided. The police did not respond to the first or the second phone call from the reporter. But when the reporter threatened to write them up, the police decided to take action. Doc Taylor, who was the Warden of Carleton County Council and the Reeve of Osgoode, had just left the building and George Drew and Don Morrow were on their way out when the police arrived.

The very embarrassing story appeared in the newspapers on a Saturday in June. Ella and I went to church the next day, as usual. Actually, Ella didn't want to go because of the publicity, but we went. It was difficult, but we went.

After Doc Taylor heard what happened, he said, "Don't worry about it. I will fix it." When the reporter attended the next meeting of Carleton County Council, Warden Taylor, stood up and said, "Gentlemen, this place is filled with rats and one just walked in. We will be going into Committee of the Whole now!" The meetings were held in-camera for quite sometime after.

Memories of Aubrey Moodie

In the early 1960's when I was being interviewed for the job of police officer, Aubrey Moodie wondered why anyone would leave a $6,000 per year job to come to work for $3,000 per year as a policeman. I told him it was for the security of the job and he sort of smiled. He never did tell me that there was no pension at the time.

Bob Mancuso

Memories of Aubrey Moodie

I was appointed as the Pontiac-Buick-GMC dealer in Manotick in September 1965 by General Motors. After surveying the area, it was decided that the northeast corner of River Road and County Road 8 was the most suitable location for the dealership. The property, which we had been told was suitably zoned, turned out not to be, so we were required to petition the residents.

Getting a new business started is quite a challenge; an address is mandatory. Dale and Ken Davidson were agreeable to letting us work out of Kendale Garage on River Road behind the airport. They didn't know what we were getting into.

New vehicles started arriving, sales got going, trades came in, new cars were pre-serviced, trades were re-conditioned, the office was overrun and the surrounding property was filled with cars. A new office building was built and a few months went by. All the time, Earl Armstrong, the Gloucester Council and the Ontario Municipal Board provided a few more challenges.

From the beginning, I had been partial to a 12-acre triangular location on Highway 16 at County Road 13 (Jockvale Road). The owner, Pat Bergin, wasn't sure he could part with it. He still pastured cattle there. Highway 16, two lanes and light traffic were no problem.

All the while, the Nepean Reeve, one Aubrey Moodie kept saying, "Come to Nepean, Jack. We will get you settled." Finally, after about six months of frustration, I called another old friend Norm Mullholland on a Saturday night. He owned six-and-a-half acres just down the road. Norm agreed to sell and we agreed on a price, all this time on the phone – a gentlemen's agreement.

Sunday morning with the GM representative in tow, we landed in Aubrey Moodie's living room. Ella let us in. I think Aubrey was still in pajamas. We agreed that I would buy dinner at Bruce McDonald's Hotel on Carling Avenue Monday at 6 p.m. Aubrey brought Grant Carman, his Planning Director, and some other Councillors. I brought Ken Murchison, my lawyer. We got along well.

The late George King of Kinell Construction started digging the footings Tuesday morning. We moved our sales office over from Gloucester the next day and serviced our cars in the Fina Station on Merivale Road.

We moved into our new building that September. God bless Aubrey Moodie. Why can't we get things done that quickly these days?

Jack May

P.S. A year or so later, Pat Bergin decided Highway 16 traffic was getting too heavy for his cows so he sold me the triangle.

Protecting the Rights of Property Owners

The Township of Nepean faced many challenges during the 1950's – none the least of which was the 1950 annexation by the City of Ottawa and the subsequent reorganization of services and delivery mechanisms. There was yet one more challenge – this one a challenge to the rights of landowners.

In 1927, the Federal Government established a federal district consisting of 899.7 square miles (2,330 square kilometers) ostensibly to forge a world-class identity for Canada's capital. It also created the Federal District Commission (FDC). Beginning in 1937, the FDC maintained and landscaped federal lands. A masterplan, developed by consultant Jacques Gréber in 1950, at the behest of Prime Minister MacKenzie King on behalf of the FDC, was intended to co-ordinate planning and development in the national capital area. The removal of the railway lines from downtown, the acquisition of farmland and forests to accommodate federal projects and institutional uses, and the creation of a 77.23 square mile (200 square kilometres) Greenbelt to control urban sprawl were key elements of the Gréber Plan.

The proposed creation of the Greenbelt, which cut through Nepean Township, caused a great deal of upset in Nepean throughout the 1950's. The Greenbelt was intended to prevent urban sprawl and provide controlled development and locations for institutional, commercial and industrial facilities. Initially, the FDC made no provision for compensation. Nepean Council took the position that the Greenbelt would not stop urban sprawl.

The FDC quietly began a program of land assembly in the 1950's for many projects such as the Defence Research Board at Shirley's Bay, the creation of a scenic parkway system and shoreline restoration and in 1954, the expropriation of over 400 acres between Woodroffe Avenue and Greenbank Road for use by Public Works Canada.

Notwithstanding the fact that the Gréber Plan and Greenbelt recommendations were not yet embodied in federal legislation, the FDC's vision was supported by the Ottawa Planning Area Board (OPAB) which also had planning approval authority. The Gréber Plan was also endorsed by Central Mortgage and Housing Corporation which approved mortgages for the developments. Local municipalities approved subdivision plans and created zoning.

We attended many meetings with the FDC at the Armories in Hull. After several meetings, it became apparent that the FDC planned to enforce the proposed Greenbelt by restricting uses through municipal zoning. Nepean Council took exception. Nepean Council, representing the interests of farmers who owned the land, was not prepared to impose the necessary zoning because it would reduce property values and prevent farmers from selling their lands to developers.

In 1956, rural ratepayers represented by Gordon Greer, Mr. Hammill and Clifford Moodie recommended Nepean Council present a brief to a Joint Parliamentary Committee appointed to make recommendations to the FDC. The brief was prepared by lawyer Richard A. Bell. We worked hard to represent the rights of citizens and argued that development would leap-frog over the Greenbelt. In fact, developers were busy acquiring land on that basis. We believed the Greenbelt boundary ought to have started at Eagleson Road. We repeatedly demanded proper compensation for property owners in the event the Federal Government proceeded with the Greenbelt land assembly.

The FDC was not prepared to offer compensation to landowners. We refused to co-operate with the Federal Government on the zoning issue.

These were trying times. Subdivision approvals also were being affected. At one point, Doug MacDonald, an FDC senior planner said there were enough registered lots inside the proposed Greenbelt lands to serve the city for the next 25 years. The matter came to a head when Larry Armstrong, a local builder in Nepean, made application to the OPAB for his Merivale Gardens subdivision. The OPAB, which supported the recommended Greenbelt plan, turned down his application. Nepean Township Council advised Larry to appeal the decision to the Ontario Municipal Board (OMB). Nepean Council supported Larry and the OMB ruled in his favour.

We had effectively defeated the plan to use local zoning as the tool to create the Greenbelt. It was the straw that broke the camel's back.

When the Federal Government finally enacted the National Capital Act of 1958, the size of the federal district was doubled to 1799.4 square miles (4,660 square kilometres), taking in parts of Ontario and Quebec. The federal district became known as the national capital region. In 1959, the FDC was replaced by the National Capital Commission (NCC) which had a mandate to implement the Gréber Plan.

Land assembly by the NCC, through expropriation, began in earnest but the price was to be negotiated. Most landowners settled on the basis of $1,000 an acre. Property values for lands within the Greenbelt were less than those for lands outside of the Greenbelt. The difference was $1,000 per acre inside the Greenbelt vs. the $2,000 to $3,000 per acre offered by land speculators to those owning land outside the Greenbelt. Most farmers accepted the compensation because they didn't want to incur more legal costs. Some of them invested in new farm land holdings. Others challenged it in court and lost.

Some farmers – including my brother Clifford, Harold Nesbitt who owned the land in Bells Corners that became home to Northern Electric (the forerunner to Nortel), and the Henrys who owned the land next to Silver Springs Farm at Baseline and Richmond Road – believed that they were not properly compensated for their lands because of the Greenbelt designation. By 1961, all of the lands yet to be acquired for Greenbelt use were subject to expropriation.

Two years later, in December 1963, we met with representatives from Northern Electric to talk about permits required to locate its buildings within the Greenbelt in Nepean. My heart wasn't in it. It was a difficult spot to be in because I believed citizens like Harold Nesbitt hadn't been treated fairly. On the other hand, development meant there was assessment for Nepean.

The reality was citizens never expected the Greenbelt to be used for anything other than conservation purposes. That confusion has caused no end of upset over the years. That perception is exacerbated by the fact that expropriated land generated revenues for the NCC. Today, when you re-negotiate leases on sites within the Greenbelt, the rates are based on market value. I believe the families, who originally owned the land, should share in the profits.

Financing Development in Nepean

The Bayshore area poised for development in the 1960's
(Ottawa City Archives, CA 8841)

The Bayshore area in the 1970's
(Ottawa City Archives, CA 9757)

Nepean was poised for development. Farmers and small builders formed the nucleus of the development industry in the early 1950's. But as the decade progressed and more government requirements were imposed, they would be replaced by larger, development companies.

Nepean's water and sewers systems had been annexed to the City of Ottawa in 1950. Unserviced, largely rural lands remained. The Province of Ontario required unserviced lots to be large enough to provide sufficient space for wells and septic systems (15,000 square feet based on a 100-foot frontage).

In the early 1950's, subdivision plans had been registered for the Meadowlands area, Carleton Heights and Fisher Heights – the latter owned by Harry Leikin. Harry didn't like the idea of the large lots because he was concerned about the future costs of servicing. After discussing it, Nepean Council approved his development on the basis that a house would be built on one half of each lot leaving the remaining half to be severed once it was serviced by water and sewer.

In 1956, Central Mortgage and Housing Corporation (CMHC) decided to discourage development on unserviced lands. A central water distribution system for any project of 100 or more houses was a mandatory condition of loan approval. As well, sewers were going to be required. This caused an exodus of some small subdividers from the business. Water areas were created by bylaw. Subdividers were responsible for the construction of the distribution system and the pumphouse which were then deeded over to the Township. Township staff were responsible for maintenance and billing. Developers were beginning to pay for more and more of the infrastructure costs.

We ran into a stumbling block in 1959 when the Ontario Municipal Board (OMB) put a freeze on development. The problem, according to the OMB Chairman J.A. Kennedy, was we had water but no sanitary sewer. Without the necessary infrastructure, Nepean would never grow, he said.

I lay awake in bed, one night, trying to figure out how to overcome the problem. I did not want to raise property taxes to cover the capital costs associated with new developments, nor could we issue debentures because of the freeze. A solution could be found if developers would agree to pay the costs of the sewage treatment plant and trunk sewers – pro-rated on the number and type of units they planned. Without this kind of co-operation, they couldn't proceed with development and Nepean could not grow.

I had an excellent relationship with Minto's Irving Greenberg of Minto which is why I presented my lot levy proposal to him. An estimated $300 charge would be payable to the Township by the developer for each new residential unit to cover the sewer costs associated with the development. That would generate the $2 million we needed to build the plant. Minto agreed with the lot levy concept as did Bill Teron, Lloyd Francis, Don Sim, and Jack Aaron and C. Mahoney. I took the proposal to Nepean Township Council and they agreed. An additional $150 per lot was levied soon after for water infrastructure. The lot levy costs were and continue to be passed on to the new homeowners as part of the sale price.

That was how lot levies were introduced in Nepean and for the first time, in Ontario. Lot levies, known as development charges today, provided us with financial stability in that the Township did not have to issue debentures to cover the costs of new growth and we avoided the large swings in taxes that would occur if the cost had been transferred to property taxes. That method of financing generated a stability that carried forward into the remainder of the century. The City of Nepean's Consolidated Statement of Operations: Sources of Financing for the year ending 1999 showed development charges and subdividers' contributions at $7.7 million in 1999 and $10.6 million in 1998.

Often when I was in Toronto, I would make a point to drop in early in the morning – without an appointment – to see the OMB Chair Mr. Kennedy. I kept my visits short and to the point. I remember the morning I dropped in to tell him about the development charges plan. I knew he was a hockey fan, so we talked hockey first. The Toronto Maple Leafs had won the night before. Then I said, "I've got what I think is good news. You may not think it is, but I think it is. I have the money to construct the sewer plant, so will you remove the freeze on development?"

"Aubrey, I never thought Nepean would survive, but you are so determined, I will give you all of the support I can,"

Mr. Kennedy, OMB Chair

I proceeded to explain the plan to generate funds by imposing development charges.

"Aubrey, I never thought Nepean would survive, but you are so determined, I will give you all of the support I can," Mr. Kennedy replied. Shortly after, the development freeze was lifted.

The development charge fee covered sewage disposal facilities, water and other services. Subdivision agreements outlined the requirements to install sanitary sewers, water mains, roads, a donation of five per cent of each subdivision for parkland and a few years later, roads, curbs and storm sewers. Developers also had to make provision for land to sell to schools boards and churches. The latter was and is at the discretion of those institutions. Later, development charges were used to cover the costs of some of the growth-related soft services such as recreation which I will talk about in *Chapter 13: Returning to Municipal Politics.*

We hired Nepean's first planner, T. Harold Charnley. We encountered another stumbling block in the early 1960's when the OMB limited the number of building permits that could be issued to 1,000 per year. That meant we had to split up the permits among the builders. There were two reasons for this: the OMB didn't want housing to get ahead of facilities such as schools and the OMB was annoyed with us because construction of Fisher Heights Public School had started without obtaining its approval to debenture it. For some reason, the request for debenture approval had not been initiated by the Clerk-Treasurer. I had to go to Toronto to arrange for a private member's bill to obtain permission to issue the debenture. The Minister of Municipal Affairs Fred Cass was particularly annoyed and didn't hesitate to chastise me. "When is the Reeve of Nepean going to learn that he has to abide by the rules and regulations?" he asked.

Just as we were passing on more costs to developers, they were pressuring us to reduce the size of building lots from the standard 100-foot frontage. Nepean Township Council was for large lots and against row housing. We had proposals from Jack Aaron, Minto and Robert Campeau. Councillor Grant Carman was heard to say more than once, "Nepean should stick to its policy on large lots. It will be changed over my dead body." Our zoning bylaw permitted high density housing in the form of apartment buildings at Greenbank near Baseline, Crystal Beach and Lakeview.

One of the first proposals for row housing came from Ken Dale in the 1960's. The subdivision was located at Woodroffe Avenue and Majestic Street. The public wanted it. Housing was in critical demand. We had to change our way of thinking. While Council thought row housing was a cheaper form of housing, it was acceptable to the public. In the end, development charges (lot levies) had something to do with the speed in which we eventually accepted row housing. Council was looking for revenue. I never thought I would see the day that there were so many though, and particularly in Barrhaven.

Barrhaven, in hindsight, was one of the most significant developments in Nepean. While some of us know Mel Barr purchased 200 acres of land in 1959, many aren't aware of a critical intervention that occurred a few years earlier.

Public Works Canada, a landowner on Greenbank Road, planned to consolidate its holdings by closing Greenbank Road which at the time was a 66-foot gravel county road. Carleton County Council and the planners with the Federal Department of Public Works shared the view that Greenbank had no value from the perspective of the future development of Nepean. As Reeve, I had a seat on Carleton County Council. I also was member of the County of Carleton's Road Committee when the bylaw to close Greenbank was given first reading. I didn't like the idea because I knew it would landlock real estate and impede development in south Nepean so, I opposed the closing.

I could not single-handedly cause Council to reverse its direction because I had only one vote. I had a policy of never being in the forefront of issues, but I often worked behind the scenes with others to resolve issues. At my request, Pat Tierney, a concerned citizen drew up a petition, signed by hundreds of residents living in South Nepean and North Gower, asking Carleton County Council to reverse its decision. They not only signed the petition, they showed up en masse at the meeting. The decision was reversed. When Public Works Canada lost its application, it was left with the problem of how to improve access to both parcels. That problem was solved when the Department connected its properties by constructing an underpass north of Fallowfield Road. Today, Greenbank Road is the main arterial into the prospering community of Barrhaven. Now, where would we be today, without Greenbank and just what were the planners thinking about when they said Greenbank had no future use?

A few years later, in 1959, Mel Barr purchased the land in Barrhaven to build a racetrack. When he learned of the Rideau-Carleton raceway plan, Mel decided to subdivide the lands and sell lots to developers. But before Barrhaven could become a reality, sewers were a necessity.

The Federal Department of Agriculture needed to service its new animal research centre. I was the deal-maker. An agreement was struck with local developers, Minto, Jack Aaron, Sheehan, Campeau and Mel Barr. They would front-end the costs of extending the Greenbank sewer in 1964. Before connections to services could be made by other new developers, the newcomers would be obliged to pay back their share of the costs to the consortia. It's a technique Ottawa Senators owner Rod Bryden might have considered to finance the cost of the Palladium Drive interchange to the Corel Centre. The Greenbank sewer agreement enabled the extension of services to the Barr property and the birth of Barrhaven in the mid 1960's. Today, the Barrhaven area is home to more than 38,000 residents.

During the heavy growth that took place in the 1960's, Nepean Council negotiated an agreement with Kanata's Reeve John Mlacek and Goulbourn's Reeve Reggie Faulkner to include their municipalities in the servicing area for the Watts Creek sewage treatment plant.

We purposely built the Watts Creek sewage treatment facility close to the Kanata municipal boundaries because we knew we needed some help to finance it and Kanata and Goulbourn needed the plant to enable development to proceed. We had a deal. Without that agreement, the growth in those areas would not have occurred at the time. But that isn't acknowledged when people talk about Kanata today.

On another occasion, I worked with a group that made an application for a television licence. It was headed by Joe Feller, the clothier. The other group was led by Ernie Bushnell. Ernie was successful and the first thing he had to do was look for a site for his station, CJOH. CJOH went on air in March 1961, broadcasting from temporary studios at Bayswater Avenue and Somerset Street. I invited Ernie to locate his station in Nepean. He was interested, but only if we could supply the services.

We had water as close as Shoppers City at Woodroffe, but we needed to get it over to Merivale to the site. The residents in Cityview weren't happy because they didn't have access to piped water, so I met with them. As an interim step, I promised to put taps in on every second street for drinking water purposes. Residents could continue to use their wells for laundry. I suggested residents petition for a local improvement or wait for the eventual installation of water mains as part of impending municipal government restructuring. They agreed with the interim measure and CJOH had a new home. Ernie Bushnell also wanted to have the address as 1313 Merivale Road, but that just wasn't possible. So we settled on 1500 Merivale Road. CJOH is going strong 42 years later.

We had our share of difficulties too.

There were other situations...such as the Sunday flood on Quinpool Crescent in Lynwood. Culverts and ditches carried away rainwater and water draining from nearby swamp lands. During construction, a bulldozer operator pushed down a pipe. The contractor jacked it up and put a post underneath to support it. What happened next? Old Christmas trees, carried along by spring run-off, jammed up against the post. That made it function like a beaver dam, causing water to back-up for miles. Heavy rains caused flooding in the basement of one of the homes. I received a call at home, donned my rubber boots and heavy clothes, called the works foreman and proceeded to have the culvert repaired and the water redirected to Moodie Drive. The homeowners were very grateful.

Then there was the woman from Lynwood who was upset about drainage. "We understand your situation, and I want to assure you that we are doing the best we can," I told her. "We understand, but your best is just not good enough," she retorted. I never forgot those words.

Servicing was one part of the equation for success; the other was holding operating costs down, once you made Nepean your address whether you owned a business or were a resident. Hydro rates were the subject of a controversy in the early 1960's. Ontario Hydro supplied power at high rural rates to residents and businesses in Nepean. In fact, Ontario Hydro's customers in Nepean were paying 84% more than Ottawans who were served by their own utility.

In 1962, three citizens, who attended a meeting in Cityview called by Nepean Council to deal with complaints about Ontario

Nepean Hydro-Electric Commission members from left are: Hugh McDonald, Reg Cross, Andy Haydon, R.B. Stapleton and Martin Montague.

Hydro rates, decided to research the issue further. The efforts by Harry Hargreaves, Joseph Cotterill and Martin Montague prompted Nepean Township Council to authorize a study of the merits of establishing a Nepean-owned hydro system. Harry, Joseph, Martin, Reg Cross and Philip White prepared a business case outlining start-up costs, projections and staffing requirements. Council supported the initiative. Negotiations began in earnest with Ontario Hydro Chair Ross Strike, Q.C., who ultimately made the decision to allow us to purchase the Nepean portion of the distribution system from Ontario Hydro. This would be the first and largest purchase of inventory ever.

However, before we made a commitment, Nepean Council asked voters to have their say by holding three plebiscites. The first dealt with purchasing the system from Ontario Hydro, the second dealt with the issue of borrowing money to pay for the system and the third posed a question about electing representatives to the hydro commission. Voters overwhelmingly supported the formation of the Nepean Hydro-Electric Commission. Savings from efficiencies demonstrated by the locally controlled Nepean Hydro were passed on to Nepean customers – beginning with a 6.5 % decrease in costs the next year. Nepean Hydro, created on July 1, 1964 and financed by a $2.47 million debenture issued by the Township on Hydro's behalf, was worth over $80 million when it became part of Hydro Ottawa in 2001. Harry, Joseph, Martin, Joseph and Reg deserve credit for doing their homework.

Nepean Hydro had offices at two locations on Merivale Road before new offices were built at 1970 Merivale Road. The foundation of the new building was constructed five feet below ground so it would be level with an anticipated railway grade separation. Otherwise, the new building, we were told, would not be aesthetically pleasing if it stood six feet higher than the reconstructed road. The bad news was the grade separation was never constructed and the hydro building flooded several times. A very costly sewer system was installed to correct the situation. At the time the Merivale grade separation was proposed, provisions also were made to construct a railway overpass at Woodroffe Avenue, Greenbank Road and Cedarview Road. The Cedarview improvement did not go forward.

The Hydro Commission and its staff made a substantial contribution to Nepean by providing good service and reduced rates. The Hydro Commission's programs were innovative. The recommendation to have developers bury hydro and telephone lines for safety and aesthetic reasons was one example. Another was the 1967 Centennial program – Light Up Nepean – in which lawn lights were installed on residential front lawns at Hydro's cost. The homeowner paid the power bill.

Playing the Game with Charlotte

Aubrey Moodie addressing an audience at a civic ceremony. From left are: Ottawa Mayor Dr. Charlotte Whitton, Nepean Township Councillors Grant Carman, Maurice Davidson and Ken Kerr and Medical Officer of Health Dr. Douglas.

Dr. Charlotte Whitton was the Mayor of Ottawa from 1951 to 1956 and from 1960 to 1964. She also served as alderman for Capital Ward from 1967 to 1972. Now Charlotte was known to be testy by times. But you had to know how to play the game with her.

Others talk about having arguments with Mayor Charlotte Whitton. I like to refer to them as discussions. Some say she kept a loaded gun in her desk drawer. I never had occasion to see it!

In the early days, Mayor Whitton was determined to renovate the County Court House, located at the corner of Daly Avenue and Nicholas Street. Carleton County Council held its meetings at the Court House

Charlotte Whitton's view was "no development outside the Greenbelt."

and operated the jail. Most of Carleton County Council members wanted to build a new court house. We had to come to some agreement because the County and the City had a cost-sharing agreement.

Stretching tax dollars was a way of doing business. As a member of the Property Committee for the Court House, we looked at every possible way to reduce operating costs and specifically, for the jail. Using the tender process, we cut costs in half for bread and buns by settling on delivery of day-old bread. Bakeries would deliver the day's surplus to us in the evening. Vegetables, such as turnips and potatoes, were purchased from local farmers, not from wholesalers. I don't know if the people in jail knew it, but nobody complained.

It was important to verify if Charlotte's view on renovating the Court House was shared by Ottawa City Council because it was the more expensive option. I wasn't sure that it was the right thing to do. I arranged a meeting with the Ottawa Board of Control's C.E. Pickering. Mr. Pickering told me he agreed that a new court house should be built, but Charlotte was so determined. He also said he disagreed with the funding arrangement but respected the fact that it was legislated. I eventually agreed with Charlotte on this issue to ensure I received support on other issues. Otherwise, we would be fighting each other for years. The Court House was renovated over a period of one year and at considerable expense. But Charlotte got her way.

Another one of Charlotte Whitton's big beefs was the way the Ottawa Suburban Road Commission (OSRC) was funded. The OSRC was set up to make decisions on construction and rehabilitation of major roads outside the old City of Ottawa and throughout the County of Carleton from Vernon to Kinburn. The funding formula was 25% from the City of Ottawa, 25% from Carleton County, and 50% from the Province of Ontario. Carleton County Council approved the budget.

Site inspections of the major roads in Carleton County took place three days in the spring and three days in the fall. Every reeve and deputy-reeve would gather at the County Court House and we would go from there. We drove from one end of Carleton County to another to assess the roads. Art Rabb, the OSRC engineer, and our own engineers accompanied us to provide us with technical advice. At night, we would meet for dinner and agree on the road priorities for the next year. Our way of doing business was one of the great advantages of Carleton County Council.

Water supply was another issue. When development was taking place during the 1950's, Central Mortgage and Housing refused to approve further development in Nepean until a central water supply was established. CMHC was determined to address the prevalence of wells and septic tanks in the Ottawa area.

The first central water supply system was constructed in Parkwood Hills as close to the City of Ottawa's boundary as possible. That way, we reasoned, we would be in good position to connect to the water system, frequently touted by Ottawa Mayor Whitton as being intentionally overbuilt to serve the needs of Nepean when it became part of Ottawa. We had pumping stations at Norice Street and another in Lynwood in Bells Corners and they were working to capacity.

That reminds me of the day that I was driving by the corner of Woodroffe Avenue and Baseline Road. There stood a group of very happy Ottawa City Councillors watching as the sod was being turned to begin the construction of the Ontario Vocational Centre – the predecessor to Algonquin College. The ceremony culminated a land search by the Province of Ontario for a suitable college location somewhere between Arnprior and Hawkesbury. Local politicians from one end of the corridor to the other were scrambling for the honours. I wanted that college. Fortunately, I didn't have to do a darn thing. Ottawa Mayor Whitton was so anxious to have the college that she offered to donate a parcel of land owned by her brother-in-law Frank Ryan. I was delighted because the land was in Nepean.

Now, my Council was pretty upset about not being invited to the ceremony. I asked them to bide their time until the project was a little further along. There would come a time when the project team would need a water connection. At the time, the Township of Nepean was served by a central water system facilitated by pump houses. The closest pump house in Nepean was on Norice Street, off Woodroffe Avenue and south of Baseline Road. This situation was an opportunity to extend our water system along Woodroffe to the college. So, I waited. When the application was made to the City of Ottawa, some red-faced officials realized the error and made application to Nepean.

Shortly after, our MPP Erskine Johnston called me to tell me the Minister of Public Works was livid. He demanded to know "What the hell kind of a Reeve do we have, that we can't get an agreement on this." Erskine assured him that I was a very fine Reeve and a reasonable man.

Within 48 hours we had an agreement. Nepean's Water Division employees would become employees of the City of Ottawa's Water Division.

"There was no question that we were going to supply them with a water connection," I replied.

"Why did you let them go so far without telling them about the water?" he asked.

"We wanted the college and just wanted to make sure they wouldn't pull out!" I replied.

I got what I wanted because Charlotte did it all for me! The trades' school was officially opened in 1965. In 1967, the school and the Eastern Ontario Institute of Technology merged into present day Algonquin College.

Nepean's Water Division became a part of the City of Ottawa's Water Division shortly after a tragic accident occurred at one of our pumping stations.

One very warm day, a Township of Nepean employee went in to inspect the pumping station on Norice Street. While he was there, the station blew up and unfortunately, he was killed instantly. I was at the township offices when this occurred.

Apart from dealing with the shock of the unfortunate death of an employee and offering support to his young family, we also had to restore the water supply quickly for health and safety reasons. I called Charlotte Whitton immediately, to explain why we needed to connect into the City of Ottawa's water system. She told me we had no business trying to run a township without water services. I became very annoyed. I told her she didn't own the water, she just processed it. I also threatened to report her to the Ontario Water Resources Commission of which I was a member.

I called our Fire Chief Leo Driscoll right away and ordered him to attach a hose to the City of Ottawa's fire hydrant on Fisher Avenue and to run it to the pumping station in Parkwood Hills. Once that was completed, I called Charlotte back to tell her what I had done and suggested she place a meter on the hydrant to track and bill water we were using. I also encouraged her to meet to discuss the situation. Within 48 hours, we had an agreement. Nepean Water Division employees would become employees of the City of Ottawa's Water Division. Ottawa would bill Nepean for the water it used and for a percentage of the capital costs.

Later, when Regional Government was formed in 1969, the responsibility for the supply and distribution of water became its responsibility. At the time, wells continued to be the source of the water supply for homes in parts of Nepean.

Just before Regional Government was formed, every community association in Nepean not only demanded access to piped water services, they wanted it to happen within one year. Before we could do anything, we needed permission from the Ontario Municipal Board (OMB) to issue a $3 million debenture. I didn't think it was possible to meet the citizens' requests for water within the one-year time-frame. I formed a committee of four or five citizens including the Medical Officer of Health Dr. Douglas who made a presentation to the OMB on our behalf.

The committee was formed because I wanted to generate some support. By enabling citizens to experience the process and letting them listen to the verdict first-hand, they could judge for themselves whether Council had worked effectively on their behalf. One of the arguments, presented by Dr. Douglas, suggested some Nepean residents were being exposed to a potentially deadly situation. The OMB's vice-chair Stan Greenwood retorted with, "Dr. Douglas, if what you say is true, the citizens of Nepean should be immune by now but we will approve the project over three years." The fact that the decision to spread the work over three years came from the OMB made it easier for residents to accept than had it come from me.

Charlotte Whitton's view was "no development outside the Greenbelt." We had plenty of discussions about that and other issues over the years.

In the early 1960's, the Township of Nepean was becoming one of Ontario's fastest growing communities and it was also fending off yet another threat of annexation. It started with a threat by Ottawa Mayor Charlotte Whitton to annex Nepean if we didn't rescind our shopping hours bylaw or at least match it with Ottawa's. Stores in Nepean had the option of staying open in the evening with the exception of Sunday, when stores were closed. Who was going to tell business people when to open and when to close their stores? They knew how to run their businesses which is why we didn't interfere by imposing strict controls on them. Charlotte saw our position as a drain on Ottawa's market share. It was a real thorn in her side. That didn't help advance good public relations with Ottawa.

That reminds me of a story about the action taken by one of our staff members who was annoyed with the owners of a retail store because they hadn't paid their municipal taxes. Its head office was based in Toronto which made collection of the debt difficult. Without discussing the situation with Council, the staff member sent in the bailiff to the local store and commandeered the cash registers. He planned to operate the cash registers until the tax arrears were covered. I was in Toronto with Alvin Stewart for the day. The furious owners managed to meet me before I left Toronto. When I boarded the plane to go home, I had a certified cheque in my pocket.

Charlotte was often quoted as saying Nepean couldn't possibly survive. Her call for annexation of Nepean Township lands between the City of Ottawa border and the Greenbelt in 1962 sent shockwaves throughout the Township. Ottawa's appetite for land and assessment was insatiable.

Had the annexation gone forward, it would have been the 10th since 1889 and reduced Nepean's population from 41,000 to 5,000. At the time, Nepean's per capita debt was less than Ottawa's. Instead, the Ontario Government commissioned the Jones Report – which set the wheels in motion for municipal government reform later in the 1960's.

Shortly after I lost the municipal election in 1969, I was honoured at a testimonial dinner attended by friends and supporters. One of the speakers, Claude Bennett, quoted Charlotte as saying – "Mr. Moodie is a stubborn, bullheaded man, out to get everything he can for Nepean and then some. He would take every dime out of your pocket. He was the worst man that I ever dealt with, terrible and I love him."

When I think back to the days of Charlotte Whitton, it is no wonder she would get upset at Nepean because we did get more than what we paid for through taxes. I think I can say, though, our relationship was based on respect. I was asked to be a pallbearer at her funeral.

We had some exciting years.

Reaching New Milestones

In November 1966, the new Nepean Township Hall, at 3825 Richmond Road, was opened officially by left, the Minister of Municipal Affairs, the Hon. J.W. Spooner, MPP and Reeve Moodie. All township departments were now housed under one roof.

Change was in the wind. On December 15, 1964, I held a special meeting of Nepean Township Council to inform Council of a submission to the Right Honourable Lester B. Pearson, Prime Minister of Canada by the Warden of Carleton County Council Earl Armstrong, Ottawa Mayor Charlotte Whitton and me. We were incensed because the National Capital Commission and Central Mortgage and Housing had hired planning consultants to prepare plans for the development and zoning of the National Capital Region outside the Greenbelt.

The two senior levels of government were also seeking special dispensation from the Province of Ontario to complete and file the plans without discussions with the City of Ottawa, the Townships of Gloucester and Nepean, Eastview and the Ottawa Planning Area Board each of which had statutory legislated planning authority. The intent was to bypass the municipalities and to work directly with the Murray Jones who was commissioned by the Province of Ontario to examine the future of local government.

We demanded the immediate suspension of work and the institution of proper procedures and consultation with municipal authorities.

Notwithstanding that intervention, the Jones Report, released in 1965, proposed the creation of a two-level metro government with boundaries as far west as Arnprior – to centralize planning, and the creation of one school board and one hydro utility.

The threat of annexation and the Jones Report influenced the Ontario Municipal Board's (OMB) view of Nepean's applications for project approvals. For example, in August 1965 – 15 years after the last annexation by Ottawa, we were still operating in cramped quarters at the old Westboro Township Hall on Richmond Road. It was time to build a new township hall to accommodate our new police department and to provide proper facilities for staff. In fact, when it rained, our engineer had to lift his feet up off the floor to keep them dry when he was in his office. Rental space was not an option because sufficient space wasn't available.

When we filed for debenture approval to construct the new township hall, the OMB responded negatively because changes to local government were impending. Our future was in question. We countered by filing photographic evidence of office conditions and presented strong arguments to support the benefits of housing our police department and holding cells and the fire department under one roof. We succeeded. The OMB approved the debenture. The new township hall in Bells Corners was going to be built. We had a future.

A commemorative brochure recounts it this way: "On January 1, 1950, the City of Ottawa annexed 7,420 acres of Nepean, almost two and a half times the total acreage annexed in the previous eighty years. The Township

Nepean's 1966 Township Council from left were: Councillor J.K. Kerr, Councillor G.M. Carman, Reeve Moodie, Deputy-Reeve E.I. Hall, Councillor W.C. Koops, and Township Clerk D.E. Hobbs.

was left as an almost exclusively rural municipality. That it would continue as such was the general expectation. But Phoenix-like, Nepean has prospered and grown.

The extent of the development is graphically shown by the fact that in 1950, the population was 2,500 with an assessment of $2,674,000; in 1966, Nepean has 46,000 people and assessment of more than $61,000,000.

Nepean has added almost a classroom a week over the past five years in its elementary school system; it has built two high schools and is presently building a third; it has added more than two homes per day since 1960, and an equal number of apartments and town houses during the past three years."

All of our services were now housed in one municipal building. But there was something missing. We had great pride in our roots. The Westboro Township Hall had been the centerpiece of Nepean's municipal government for over 80 years and a very physical link with our history. Some of our staff wanted to repatriate a part of that history by relocating the bell in the belfry at the old Westboro Township Hall to the new township hall at Bells Corners. In years gone by, the bell was used to sound the fire call for volunteer fire fighters, and in much earlier days to sound the curfew. The sentimental attachment was too great; a plan came together.

Our Township Clerk David Hobbs, Fire Chief Leo Driscoll and Chief Building Inspector Bill Bourne teamed up for the mission. Now, legend has it that the *Flight of the Bell* was a midnight caper, cloaked under cover of darkness, and accomplished without the knowledge or permission of Council. That isn't quite true. Dave, Leo and Bill told me what they planned to do and when they planned to do it. I shrugged my shoulders and said, "If that's what you want to do, I have no objections." So, off they went, fire truck and all, in broad daylight, to repatriate the bell to Bells Corners Township Hall. It's a wonder no one asked them what they were doing when they pulled up in front of the Westboro building and started the process. The bell was transported back to Bells Corners, refurbished to its original glory, and prominently displayed outside the new township offices. A graphic adaptation of the bell was adopted as Nepean's corporate symbol in the early 1970's and eventually appeared on everything from stationery to advertisements to vehicle identification in Nepean's green - Pantone 555. The original bell was relocated to the new Nepean City Hall, Ben Franklin Place, 101 Centrepointe Drive in 1988.

Nepean was also celebrating the opening of two brand new arenas on October 9, 1965. They were Centennial Year projects marking Canada's 100th year as a country in 1967. The arenas would provide 10 to 12 hours of public skating each week. Sixty feet of benches were needed to seat the hockey players in the arenas and dressing rooms. (Council minutes record Reeve Moodie's agreement to look after the sawing of the pine logs for the benches. That wasn't his only contribution! Aubrey had to literally stick-handle his way through a major conflict that occurred before the arenas were built.)

Canada's Centennial was coming up and we wanted to celebrate it appropriately. Merivale was experiencing the greatest growth, but Bells Corners historically generated the hockey teams. We had received a Centennial grant to build the Merivale Arena which enraged the residents of Bells Corners! Keith Duke led the charge. The solution was to convince the entire community to help build two arenas.

I arranged a meeting with the 22 homeowners' associations in Nepean to explain the benefits of building two arenas. I was sure there would be some savings if we used the same plans, architect and contractor. I also wanted to determine if the community associations would support the construction of two arenas by spearheading the campaign to raise the funds required to build the second arena. One citizen said to me at the end of the meeting,

The Great Nepean Bell Caper

Contrary to folklore the Township of Nepean's bell, which was destined to become its corporate symbol, was spirited away from Westboro Township Hall in the middle of the day. The bell was refurbished and placed in front of the new Township offices at 3825 Richmond Road.

Reeve Moodie found time to play broomball in 1963 with Township staff.
Back row from left: Al Jenkins, John Verney, Don Bailley, Dave Mulvagh
and Bill Bourne; middle row from left: Ted Aldridge, Orval Woodroffe,
Ron Driscoll, Leo Driscoll, Dave Driscoll, Keith Davidson, Ned Hansen,
Tom Rutherford and Grant Armstrong; front row from left: Councillor
Bill Koops, Councillor Grant Carman, Reeve Moodie, Councillor J.Ken
Kerr and Township Clerk David Hobbs.

"Aubrey, I came here to oppose the plan but you have made such a strong presentation that I couldn't help but go along with you." The 22 homeowners associations agreed and successfully raised the money by launching a door-to-door campaign. We awarded one contract to construct two new arenas: Bell Centennial Arena and Merivale Centennial Arena. The arenas were built and ready for use in advance of the Centennial celebrations.

At the time, I had envisioned construction of six arenas located across the Township. Andy Haydon's dream was the construction of a large, multi-purpose facility – the Nepean Sportsplex – a landmark that continues to serve our citizens. For me, I had seen a similar complex in larger cities. However, I never dreamed of using development charges to finance recreational facilities such as the Sportsplex.

We used development charges to finance sewer, water and roads facilities and roads when the Ontario Municipal Board wouldn't approve our debenture requests. Had we not arranged financing using development charges, Nepean would not have grown. It seemed to me that as time went on, development funds were being used indiscriminately until Ontario stepped in to tighten up how they were to be used.

My comments aren't intended to criticize Andy Haydon and the Sportsplex. They just show that we had very different philosophies. I was a fiscal conservative.

Canada's Centennial in 1967 also carried with it the expectation of increased tourism and more demands for family camping sites. Camping was permitted at Lansdowne Park but Ottawa Mayor Don Reid was the recipient of numerous noise complaints from residents living in Ottawa South.

These campers were tourists and neither one of us wanted to discourage them from visiting us again. Don approached me to determine if Nepean had a location for the campsite. My preference was to work together in a partnership. We had a site on Corkstown Road and I proposed a cost-sharing agreement based on Ottawa paying two-thirds of the costs and Nepean the balance. He agreed. The new location was managed by a special committee made up of appointees from Ottawa and Nepean, known as the Ottawa-Nepean Municipal Campsite Authority. Today, the campsite is a popular choice for tourists and one that generates revenue for the city. I had the pleasure of serving as a member of the Ottawa-Nepean Campsite Board for many years after I was no longer an elected official.

The Campsite Authority was chaired by an elected official. I was often asked to serve as the Chair but I declined because I believed it was the politicians who frequently met and mingled at social functions. That was where issues were discussed and often resolved. It made for better public relations. For years, that is what worked for me.

Memories of Aubrey Moodie

I remember well the years in the 1950's when you were on Council and the Library Committee was working to establish what started out to be a school section library and ended up as a Police Village Library. It was named the Cityview Public Library until the City of Nepean was formed and it became the Nepean Public Library.

Those years were exciting as you promoted urban development and developed social programs so important to our community.

You have my thanks for the co-operation and advice you so willing supplied to all of us in the Township.

Ruth E. Dickinson

In the 1980's, Nepean City Council named Nepean Public Library's newest branch at Barrhaven the Ruth E. Dickinson Branch.

By the end of the 1960's, Nepean's public library system grew to include the Cityview Public Library, a bookmobile and the Centennial Library in Bells Corners.

(Ottawa City Archives)

Changing Structures and Leaders

Reeve Moodie conducts his final meeting as Reeve in the Nepean Township Council Chambers on December 15, 1969. From left are: Councillors Paul Friesen and Ken Kerr, Township Clerk David Hobbs, Reeve Moodie, Councillors Grant Carman, William Koops and Andy Haydon. Missing is Councillor Ed Hall.

*P*rior to the formation of Regional Government in 1969, Carleton County Council had a strong rural voice, drawing its members from a largely agricultural base. The City of Ottawa did not have representation on Carleton County Council but it did pay some of the bills. Naturally, most members of Carleton County Council opposed the plan to introduce Regional Government because it embodied elected representation from the City of Ottawa.

I had the feeling that many Nepean residents believed it was time for a change. The township's semi-rural base had evolved into an urban township and was characterized by increased demands for programs and services. The growth was phenomenal – in 1960, we had a population of 16,500. In 1969, we had topped 56,000 and were on the way to the 60,000 mark.

My colleagues believed I was the one person who could successfully lead the opposition against the formation of Regional Government. They offered me the chief executive position as Warden for Carleton County Council in return for opposing Regional Government. I already had the unprecedented distinction of serving as Warden for three terms – in 1955, 1962 and 1966 – something no other person had achieved since Carleton County Council was formed in 1842. It was an honour to be asked by your peers to serve a fourth. I declined because I thought that with the proper set-up, Regional Government just might work. I held the view that citizens believed Carleton County Council had outlived its usefulness, so I didn't offer strong resistance to Regional Government.

But I was wary. What was different about Regional Government was that, for the first time, rural and city issues would be considered by one body. I think it is fair to say that I had a desire to make the new structure work. Today, the new City of Ottawa Council is facing challenges, but no greater than what we faced.

It is true that I often worked behind the scenes on issues by encouraging groups and individuals to do their homework and to make their case. I took great care to guard against, publically, compromising my position as a member of Council. My responsibility as Council member was to look at what was best for the entire municipality. If you don't stop to listen, discuss and evaluate issues before you take a position, it becomes far more difficult to get the support of other members of Council.

You also need to offer tangible support when it is needed. In 1968, just before Regional Government was formed, Carleton County Council was cautious about allocating money for capital projects. In the spring, Hiram Wilson, Reeve of Fitzroy took us to see the county roads in his community. They were in terrible shape but he was told he would have to wait for funding. He was in a fix. I said, "Mr. Wilson, we are going into the

Regional Municipality of Ottawa-Carleton very shortly and we have a capital budget approved for reconstruction of roads in Nepean. I believe that when Regional Government is formed, we will have a better chance to access funding than you will, so we will give you part of Nepean's current allocation." That was the kind of co-operation we had.

In setting the new Council for Regional Government, Ottawa, with 75% of the population, would have only 16 of the 31 seats. The reeves and deputy-reeves from the urban townships and less populated rural townships also would serve as regional councillors. The chair was to be elected by Regional Council. It is interesting to note the population balance changed as the suburbs and rural areas became more populated such that Ottawa's population of 326,000 was less than 50% of the 730,000 residents living in the Regional Municipality of Ottawa-Carleton in the 1990's.

In the days preceding the formation of Regional Council, we had many meetings to discuss the transition, structure and responsibilities. I recall attending half a dozen meetings with Lorne Cummings, the Deputy Minister of Municipal Affairs. He never took a set of minutes. No doubt, he reported to the Minister, but we were gullible enough not to insist the discussions be recorded formally.

Determining the number of political representatives for Nepean and Gloucester was a critical decision from my perspective. Nepean and Gloucester were going to have an equal number of representatives, that is, until Gloucester Reeve Armstrong left the meeting temporarily. By the time he returned, I had convinced the group that Nepean Township's population was larger and therefore, required one more representative than Gloucester.

The new structure gave Regional Government responsibility for co-ordinated planning, debentures, assessment, water supply, trunk sewers and sewage treatment, the county road system, homes for the aged and welfare. Local municipalities retained responsibility for police, fire, local roads, local planning and local storm and sanitary sewers, library, recreation, garbage collection and recycling, bylaws, and municipal tax collection. I was particularly pleased when the responsibility for water supply and distribution was transferred from the City of Ottawa to Regional Government.

In the first years of Regional Government, it quickly became apparent it had generous access to financing. When the Province of Ontario removed the mayors and reeves from Regional Council in 1994, Ontario effectively created two separate tiers of government with no linkage between them. The wheels were set in motion to create the new City of Ottawa which we have today. We can only hope that the benefits of the new City to the taxpayers will match the promises that were made before amalgamation.

The formation of Regional Government in 1969 co-incided with my defeat to challenger and one-term Councillor Andrew S. Haydon.

In mid-June 1969, Councillor Ed Hall came to me. He was concerned that I would have an election to fight. I asked Councillor Hall and Councillor Carman if they would consider running for Reeve. They said they were too busy and they believed I would win. Even the late Hon. Walter Baker, MP for Nepean-Carleton, urged me to run. In the end, I decided I wasn't going to capitulate to a person I believed hadn't earned it.

It would be my first election since 1954 when I ran against Benny Acres for Reeve. I had been acclaimed in every subsequent election. There was only one other instance when I thought I would have to mount an election campaign. A United Church Minister from Manordale decided he was going to compete for Reeve. I thought he was a threat to me and I shared those concerns with Irving Greenberg. "I'll fix that," said Irving. "He is a New Democratic Party (NDP) member. I will tell him he should run provincially because we need him." The Minister ran for the NDP and was soundly trounced.

I was blessed because I had good people and a good organization when I needed them. Collin Collins from Lynwood was a respected, ex-military man who helped me out early in my political career. After Collin helped me, he spearheaded Walter Baker's campaign for MP Nepean-Carleton. Eventually, Collin moved on to orchestrate provincial campaigns.

I had excellent support. Nancy Sheehan took over from Paul Friesen in running one of my campaigns; there was Pat Nash, Jim Gilfilan, John Monaghan, Don Fraser, Bob Hussey and others. Mike Anka was my financial agent in the 1950's and a strong supporter of mine.

Andy Haydon had a seat on Nepean Township Council because of an action I had taken a few years earlier. Doc (Derek) Campfield, the Lynwood Village Community Association president, was pressing for a ward system. The current electoral process required Councillors to be elected at-large, by all eligible voters in Nepean who chose to cast their ballots. I was opposed to the ward system because I believed councillors elected from a ward would favour their electors instead of considering what was best for the whole township. As a compromise, I approached Erskine Johnston, MPP, to seek the Ontario Government's permission to add two more members to Council. We went from a five to a seven member Council. Andy Haydon ran in that election and won.

Andy was the newcomer who had one three-year term on Nepean Council. A headline appearing in The Ottawa Citizen on Saturday, November 29, 1969, positioned the contest this way: "Nepean's old guard vs. the young Turks. The captions read: "Reeve Aubrey Moodie's strength: His bond with township's pioneer stock - Challenger Andrew Haydon finds audience among the newcomers."

Nepean's old guard vs. the young Turks:

"Reeve Aubrey Moodie's strength: His bond with township's pioneer stock - Challenger Andrew Haydon finds audience among the newcomers."

While some suggested Andy didn't have a chance against me, my feeling was that there was no hope of me winning the 1969 election. People weren't happy because sewers were overloaded and their basements were flooding. We had many new residents. The two million dollars we had in the bank couldn't be spent because the Ontario Government had frozen all expenditure approvals until Regional Government was formed.

I was very aware of the dynamics. What I had to offer, as a fiscal conservative, was 15 years of progress as Reeve. When I became Reeve in 1954, the population was just over 7,000. There wasn't one single paved county road in the township. We didn't have a fire department or a police department. There was no such thing as a recreation department or public facilities. Libraries didn't exist. We had no hospital. We had no water or sewage systems. We had a few schools. We had one staff member.

By 1969, our population was one its way to 60,000 – the largest increase of 40,000 occurred in the 1960's making us one of the fastest growing municipalities in Ontario. There is no doubt we had growing pains but we managed them. By 1969, all of our main roads (approximately 50 miles) were paved. We had our own fire department and our own police department. Our recreation department operated programs out of facilities that included two arenas funded by community fund-raising and provincial grants, tennis courts and four outdoor swimming pools. Our township library system was supplemented by a bookmobile which toured through various communities. We had excellent public and separate elementary schools and secondary schools. We had a reliable water and sewer system – the latter funded through my development charge plan – and without which we would not have been permitted to grow. A new township hall replaced the one annexed by Ottawa and senior citizens had a home for the aged at Carleton Lodge.

The race for Reeve in the autumn of 1969 was a hard fought battle. I lost. The vote was: 9,099 to 4,681.

Taking a Political Respite

Aubrey and Ella Moodie were honoured at a testimonial dinner. Friends celebrated Aubrey's contributions as Reeve from 1954 to 1969 and as Councillor from 1950 to 1954 and thanked Ella by acknowledging her support. In encouraging well-wishers to support the new Township Council, Aubrey quipped, "This is not my last political will and testament!"

Almost 1,000 friends and supporters gathered to pay tribute to Aubrey and his wife Ella at a testimonial dinner in February 1970. Aubrey returned the praise and admiration graciously and encouraged the well-wishers to support the new Council but he also added, "This is not my last political will and testament."

Provincial Minister of Finance and Commercial Affairs Bert Lawrence, Minister of Municipal Affairs Darcy McKeough, Minister of Highways George Gomme, and Minister of Transport Irwin Haskett were among the guests. Ontario Premier John Robarts, in a message wired to organizers, said Mr. Moodie was "one of the finest men Eastern Ontario has ever developed...and one of the best known municipal figures in the province."

The Ottawa Journal in its March 2, 1970 edition, described Moodie as a man who had to "leave school in the depression and earn his way with his hands and his heart."

We were joined by many friends that evening. Proceeds from the dinner were donated to the Queensway-Carleton Hospital Building Fund. That evening, I made a public commitment to create a $200 bursary to be presented in my name for 60 years, to the Carleton Board of Education (CBE) secondary school student who achieved the highest marks. A plaque, suggested by Councillor Grant Carman who knew how I felt about the value of education, was unveiled that evening. I receive thank you letters from students most years. It is very gratifying. The CBE is now known as the Ottawa-Carleton District School Board (OCDSB). Today, the bursary is being managed on my behalf by the Bells Corners United Church. I have an agreement with the Church and they have the money. That's because I wasn't impressed with the way the OCDSB Chair handled the Board meeting at which I attended to present the bursary.

The change in 1969 was good in some ways. Andy brought new ideas to the table.

Andy Haydon and I had different views on how development charges should be used. One of the first changes made by Andy was to allocate a part of the development charges to recreation instead of relying solely on the tax base. I believed development charges should be used for core services, not for recreational facilities such as the Nepean Sportsplex. That is not to say I didn't support recreation. I had envisioned six covered arenas strategically located in the township.

Andy's vision for the controversial multi-use sports facility was unveiled in 1971 and the Nepean Sportsplex opened in June of 1973. It has since become a landmark and a popular location for everything from competitive sports to physical fitness, visual arts and shows.

Expropriation of waterfront along the Ottawa River and the Jock River to preserve the shores and rivers for public use was another Haydon initiative which frankly I didn't support at the time. I wasn't in favour of purchasing land on speculation. I appreciate his vision today because waterfronts are accessible for the enjoyment of many citizens.

It was a very interesting time for me after my defeat as Reeve and before I was re-elected to serve as a Councillor in 1973-74 and again in 1975-76. Many people continued to call me for advice.

Returning to Municipal Politics

Councillor Bob Mitchell, left and Aubrey Moodie

The township, under Andy's leadership, was moving ahead on a number of issues including the acquisition of land for the Merivale Acres Industrial Colony (the first municipally-owned business park in the region) when I was re-elected to the 1973-74 Nepean Township Council. I received 5,867 votes, just 157 votes behind Councillor Bob Mitchell who topped the polls. Reeve Haydon and Deputy-Reeve Grant Carman were acclaimed.

Andy and I had many disagreements about how tax dollars were spent.

One of the issues we were at odds over was the construction of the Hunt Club Road. I was not against a secondary highway because the need was undeniable. In fact, Carleton County Council had spent considerable effort working with the Province of Ontario to design and acquire land to accommodate the road. The plan was premised on using Fallowfield Road as the base and extending it to the east by building a bridge across the Rideau River, south of the airport, and to the west by extending it to Goulbourn and Stittsville.

Andy and I also disagreed about the proposed route for Highway 416. Originally, it was to be constructed from Prescott, through the Pine Glen community with a flyover at Meadowlands Drive. The proposed road followed Merivale Road to the site of the Super Loblaws store at Merivale Road and along Merivale to the Queensway. During my tenure as Reeve, we had worked with the Ministry of Transportation and had all of the approvals in place. The 13 affected Nepean homeowners' associations also had endorsed the plan.

I found myself embroiled in a heated controversy over my land holdings in Barrhaven.

Nepean Township Council withheld the permits for a proposed high-rise condominium on Meadowlands Drive until the route was approved by Council. We issued the permits a year too soon because the next thing we knew, the residents of the condominium were objecting to the proximity of the road. The route was scrapped following my defeat in 1969.

When I announced my intention to seek re-election to Council in late 1974 for the 1975-76 term, I found myself embroiled in a heated controversy about my land holdings in Barrhaven. I was one of three partners who had purchased a 30-acre parcel of land for $32,000 in 1969 in Barrhaven. The land backed onto the railway tracks, south of Fallowfield Road and next to Greenbank Road. I was accused of one of the most serious charges a politician can face: conflict of interest.

It was a difficult election campaign because I was the subject of a very incorrect perception. In fact, Township Solicitor Richard A. Bell in 1974 had prepared an opinion after reviewing the situation. Mr. Bell declared that he could find no direct conflict of interest in the case. The City Solicitor in his legal opinion of November 19, 1974 stated, "My study of all resolutions and motions of council indicates that we may disregard at once any suggestion of direct pecuniary interest on the part of Mr. Moodie. No action was taken at any time which related directly to the property." I was the fifth of five Councillors elected, polling 5,295 votes. Reeve Haydon was acclaimed.

I took steps before that election to provide the facts by releasing a statement to the news media, extracts of which follow:

➤ In once again seeking the trust and confidence of the citizens of Nepean, I am well aware of the efforts of some to attack my integrity and my conduct as a Councillor...and specifically to charge that I have been guilty of a direct conflict of interest in various matters decided upon during meetings of the Council at which I was present.

➤ On August 9, immediately upon my return from a seminar sponsored by the Municipal Association of Ontario whereat it was suggested that even in municipalities where there were no specific declaration of interest provisions to more specifically define the provincial legislation, Councillors should declare their interest. I did so through correspondence to Reeve Haydon and made copies of this correspondence available to all members of Council.

➤ I was not present at the October 15 meeting at which. Resolution 598 dealing with Provincial aid to the housing development planned in Barrhaven was discussed. The minutes of the Township indicate clearly that I absented myself after all discussions at 9:30 p.m. and was not present for the discussion of resolution 598.

➤ On October 17, a meeting of the Township Council was called to deal with tenders relating to municipal services for the Barrhaven area, a meeting which approved tenders dealing in the millions. I was not present at these meetings because of my declared interest.

➤ I seek the trust of the people of Nepean for my commitment to careful and balanced development, continued growth and preservation of the quality of like our communities have a right to expect. I place my record of service before the people of Nepean to judge and assess. I attack no member of Council. I seek only to work with other councillors for the benefit of Nepean.

➤ My personal commitment has always meant a strict code of ethics, based on a clear respect for the public interest and insuring no personal gain from my public responsibilities. This has governed my activities in the past and will continue to do so. I await with eagerness the legal opinion sought by the Township of Nepean on the alleged conflict of interest. I am prepared to defend my conduct in every possible way.

When the matter was raised in the Provincial Legislature, I received the support of several sitting members.

The conflict of interest allegations, however, would reach a new high when the Barrhaven lands sold in 1976 for $982,750. The controversy flared up during municipal elections for the 1977-78 term of Council. Andy and I were candidates for the position of Reeve. My platform was responsible financial leadership. I was concerned about rising taxes and what I believed to be irresponsible spending on recreational facilities such as the National Capital Equestrian Park, the high operational costs of the Sportsplex, and the growing debenture debt – from $4 million in 1969 to a five-year net capital forecast for 1974-1978 requiring debentures of more than $26 million. The 1976-1980 capital forecast decreased to a net capital expenditure program of $19.3 million.

Andy Haydon said his spending was the result of my alleged misman-agement during my tenure as Reeve. He pledged that the planned borrowing had come to an end. One thing was certain: taxpayers of Nepean were angry about the property tax hikes.

Looking back, I had not figured on taxpayers supporting large tax increases and I had a different plan for recreation. It is true that the Nepean Sportsplex became a landmark for the township, but I was concerned about the plan to borrow more money for more recreational facilities. A question on the 1976 ballot dealt with the construction of an arena at Bayshore. The result was 4,011 in favour and 14,511 against.

The 1976 election campaign was a particularly difficult campaign, one that I lost because of particularly well-contrived, well-timed, political smear. The controversy, once again, centred on the purchase of a 30-acre parcel of land purchased in 1969 in Barrhaven and sold in 1976.

Someone, a person still living, took some material to The Citizen and destroyed my career.

It was a rough deal. When I went to bed one night before the election, I had the election won. When I woke up the next morning to The Citizen story, the election was lost. The headlines were on page one and my request for a provincial inquiry was buried on page 65. Voter turnout was high. The vote was 9,715 for Haydon and 8,935 for me.

When I went to bed one night before the election, I had the election won. When I woke up the next morning to The Citizen story, the election was lost.

Reeve Haydon's 1977-1978 Council consisted of incumbents Deputy-Reeve Bob Mitchell, Councillors Ben Franklin and Al Loney, and newcomers Ed Puccini, Eileen Consiglio and Margaret Rywak. Councillor Consiglio, unfortunately, passed away during her term. I was in the hospital at the time, recovering from surgery when John Monaghan and several other friends, including Bob Mitchell, dropped into to see me. Bob Mitchell asked me if I would consider letting my name stand to replace the late Councillor Consiglio. I suggested Grant Carman be considered because he was the runner-up in the last election. Bob was persistent so I agreed to let my name stand. I was advised later by a reliable source on Council that my name was not presented. Grant Carman was asked to return. Now Grant was a great Councillor. I had no qualms about his appointment, but I was really annoyed that I was asked and agreed to let my name stand, yet my interest was not communicated to Council.

I told my campaign team what had happened. They said, "We won't let Bob Mitchell away with that. If you agree, we will work against him." Prior to the 1978 municipal elections, Andy Haydon decided to leave Nepean

Township Council to seek the position of Chair of the Regional Municipality of Ottawa-Carleton. Bob Mitchell and Ben Franklin were candidates for the position of Reeve. I threw my support behind Ben Franklin. Bob was the Deputy-Reeve and was favoured to win. Bob lost. It was a settling of scores. Bob approached me a few days later. He was naturally very critical of my actions but he also went on to remind me how he had supported me over the years. After that discussion, I thought perhaps I had been a little too critical.

I don't carry a grudge. When a person pays the price, then it is over. Bob Mitchell was a good Councillor. A year or so later, a representative of the Conservative Government asked me to suggest a candidate to represent the local riding in the upcoming provincial election. I recommended Bob Mitchell. I couldn't think of anyone better than Bob. He went on to win. Bob and I have been friends every since.

One of Andy Haydon's decisions, as the Reeve, was to create a zoning bylaw for rural Nepean. I never thought farmers would accept the zoning of their agricultural lands because farmers are pretty independent. But they did.

We had one additional disagreement. I was no longer a member of Council. In the process of creating a bylaw to zone the southern half of the township, miles of land fronting on the west side of Richmond Road were zoned as flood plain. This land has never been known to flood in 100 years and it is unlikely it will flood in the next 100 years. There were many farmers affected including the Fosters, the Munroes, Garnet Ralph, Alvin Stewart and me. I strongly objected to the zoning as did my neighbours because the flood plain designation would devalue our properties.

The township's bylaw was appealed to Ontario Municipal Board and the bylaw was upheld. Alvin Stewart and I went to Toronto to meet with the Minister of Agriculture Lorne Henderson to suggest he bring the matter up before Cabinet. We wanted our lands exempted from the flood plain designation. Lorne decided he would accompany the Minister of Municipal Affairs from Brockville to view the site before he made his decision. I met them at the airport and took them on a tour to help them become familiar with the situation. As a result, they recommended to Cabinet that a new study be conducted by a different firm of consultants.

The flood plain zoning, in question, was removed. Dick Bell, who was the solicitor for the Township at the time, took strong exception to what we had done. He was particularly annoyed that no one from the Township of Nepean had been invited to take part in the flood plain inspection. I told him to continue to look after the interests of Nepean and I would look after the interests of Aubrey Moodie.

That was the way things were done: directly. If you had a problem, you could approach the Ontario Government.

When all was said, I never lost respect for Andy Haydon and our disagreements were never personal. I didn't agree with the location of the new headquarters for the Regional Municipality at Lisgar and Elgin. I thought Lansdowne Park had more merit because of the space and the community flavour. One of the best deals Andy made was obtaining the agreement by the Province of Ontario to take over the operation of the Congress Centre. Opened on November 3,1983, capital funding for the Congress Centre was provided by the Regional Municipality of Ottawa-Carleton and the Federal and Provincial Governments. Andy Haydon asked Ontario to take over the operations in early 1984. Effective April 1, 1984, Ontario agreed to operate it as an agency of the Ministry of Tourism and Recreation and to fund all operating deficits.

Andy wanted Nepean to become a city because he believed it would add to the prestige of the municipality when dealing with businesses and other levels of government. I wasn't keen on losing Township status because it meant we lost our entitlement to generous rural grants and the ability to access funds for development roads. Andy was successful. Nepean Township was elevated to city status on November 24, 1978, six days before the end of his term as Reeve. Andy was Nepean's first Mayor. He was succeeded by Ben Franklin who served as Mayor until 1997.

A Moodie Memory

Nepean was growing at a tremendous rate and individual Councillors were being contacted more frequently by citizens. The Councillors had no office space in the Township building. To deal with these issues, Deputy-Reeve Bob Mitchell requested that the Township purchase for him a portable pocket recorder so that he could voice record issues and then provide the tape to the administrative staff for resolution of the particular issues.

Reeve Andy Haydon decided that if one of the Councillors had this equipment (which cost about $400 per unit) then all Councillors should be entitled to it. Reeve Haydon then proceeded to take a poll of all members of Council. When it came to Mr. Moodie, he replied, "No thanks. I'll take the cash."

Merv Beckstead
Former Commissioner of Finance
City of Nepean

Keeping our Environment Healthy

*I had the privilege of serving on the Ontario Water Resources Commission
(OWRC) for 10 years. The OWRC was renamed the Environmental Hearing
Board when it became part of the Ontario Ministry of Environment. From
left are F.S. Hollingsworth of Sault Ste. Marie; H.E. Brown of Toronto;
J.H. Root , MPP and Vice-Chair; D.S. Caverly, General Manager; D.J. Collins,
Chair; W.S. MacDonnell, Secretary; L.E Venchiarutti, Toronto; D.A. Moodie,
Richmond and Dr. C.A. Martin of Milton.*

$\mathscr{I}$took great pride in my 10-year service as
Commissioner for the Ontario Water Resources
Commission (OWRC). Appointed by the Lieutenant-
Governor-in-Council, I was sworn-in on September
29, 1964. Premier John Robarts attended.

The OWRC was established by Premier Leslie Frost's
Government. The OWRC had broad powers to
protect and develop water supplies and systems and to
control sewage works. Ontario and local municipalities
shared the cost of the systems. I traveled from one
end of the province to the other, representing the
OWRC as a negotiator or as a panel member at

public hearings or public meetings. The rate was no more than $55 a day. Often, I was the lone member selected because of my municipal knowledge and experience. The OWRC was renamed the Environmental Hearing Board when the OWRC Act became the responsibility of the Ministry of Environment.

Public hearings were required before the OWRC could approve a municipal applications for water or sewage projects. The OWRC also had the power to force industrial and commercial businesses found negligent, to collect, treat and dispose of waste properly.

Here are a few of the more memorable environmental hearings in which I participated. The location of a hydro transmission line from Colbeck to Limebeck north of Guelph in 1975 was one. There was no other possible route according to Ontario Hydro. Property owners, including a group of people from Toronto, strongly objected and demanded a hearing. The Minister of Energy, the Hon. Dennis Timbrell agreed and the hearing was held in Hillsburgh, Ontario. The panel consisted of Dr. C.A. Martin, Dave Caverly who was Chair and me as vice-chair. Following the week-long hearing, I spent two days traveling by helicopter to visit every second farmer to discuss the proposed route, alternatives and fair compensation. They feared the new corridor would replicate the problems they were experiencing with existing corridors such as the amount of arable land rendered unproductive as a result of the corridor designation and access points.

There were also issues with television reception. I believe I gained farmers' confidence because of my agricultural background and knowledge of farm equipment. In fact, the official minutes record a commendation of my approach by one of the opposition groups. In the end, we recommended a completely different route. It saved Ontario $1 million, required less land, and ultimately, was not contentious. Residents actually wrote the Minister to thank him for the decision.

I believe we were more receptive to looking at a problem from all angles than we seem to be today.

The Government of Ontario asked the OWRC to name a representative to negotiate a cost-sharing agreement to finance a new filtration plant and a distribution system. It was needed to serve Sarnia and seven municipalities, including the rural Township of Moore, some 30 miles away. The OWRC asked me to conduct the negotiations because of my familiarity with municipal government. I worked with Mayor Blundey, a Liberal who later was elected as an MPP, and the elected officials of seven municipalities. It was quite an accomplishment to get agreement. The water filtration plant was built in Sarnia. My efforts were obviously appreciated by some because two years later, I was introduced by the Reeve of Moore Township as "the man who got us water" to a crowd of 1,000 people at the Ontario Good Roads Convention in Toronto.

In another situation, there was vociferous opposition to a water filtration plant for St. Thomas. The St. Thomas Mayor did not want his municipality to pay the bill. He didn't know the water plant was a non-negotiable stipulation in an agreement to locate a Ford Motor plant in nearby Talbotville. Ford was contributing to the cost of the plant and we were sworn to secrecy. The negotiations were long and intense, but we succeeded eventually. The plant was built near Lake Erie to serve St. Thomas and the surrounding communities including Talbotville.

He didn't know the water plant was a non-negotiable stipulation in an agreement to locate a Ford motor plant in nearby Talbotville.

Severn, Winisk and Albany were other destinations. One of the things I learned about those communities was the high degree of effort by citizens to sustain their lives. I watched some women pick moss from rock cuts to use as diapers for their babies. It made me think about how much we take for granted.

One of the gentlemen I came to know well through the OWRC was John Root. John served the OWRC in several capacities for 15 years. The OWRC had a number of studies underway in Northern Ontario including surveys of the Severn, Winisk, Albany, Moose and Attawapiskat Rivers and their tributaries. On one of my trips to Northern Ontario with John, we spent some time visiting with Father Ouimet, a parish priest at Landsdowne House located on the Attawapiskat River. Father Ouimet, who had lived in the area for 16 years, was also known for his skills as a gardener. Shortly after our visit, Father Ouimet contracted tuberculosis (TB) and died. I was given TB inoculations as a precaution.

I flew to Moosonee to sit as part of a panel to make recommendations on how to establish local government there.

Red Lake was the location of a hearing called to investigate a complaint involving industrial discharge of waste into a nearby watercourse. The hearing lasted for just two-and-a-half days. I wanted to return to Ottawa to attend a retirement party for Edgar Gamble, Reeve of Richmond. I had a flight arranged, but it wasn't going to get me home in time. Now, I am sure there would be a great outcry if anyone did today, what I did then.

Steps are being

taken to manage

landfill sites in an

environmentally-

sensitive way.

I happened to notice the company officials, who had appeared before the OWRC, were dining at the same restaurant as John Root and I. I asked John about the propriety of accompanying them to Toronto. John thought it would be perfectly okay and the officials welcomed me into their aircraft – a very luxurious jet. Once in Toronto, I was able to catch a connecting flight home. Within the space of four hours, I traveled from Red Lake to Toronto to Richmond, Ontario. I was home – on time for Edgar Gamble's reception. Looking back, taking the flight from Red Lake to Toronto was a conflict of interest.

Over the years, I have met many people on the street. One of the biggest surprises for me was the day the caretaker at the train station in Hornepayne recognized me because of our hockey days years ago. He was from Barry's Bay.

Garbage disposal methods have changed significantly over the years. In our earlier days, a private contractor held the garbage disposal contract for the Township. Eventually, the Township decided to operate its own site on Moodie Drive at Trail Road. Land was purchased from Robert Campeau. Eventually, an environmental hearing was held. The OWRC held a two-week hearing to review the plans for the future. The OWRC's Chair John

Root did not favour the location because of the soil conditions. He recommended approval to the Ministry of Environment subject to very strict conditions ranging from the use of strong liners to contain leachate to controlled traffic to the site. I was personally concerned because I had an open drain running through my farm from which cattle drank. As a result of an intervention to Environment Minister George Kerr, some of the conditions were challenged and the certificate to operate was issued.

A friend on the OWRC, Harold Browne, warned John and me that we were going to be relieved of our duties. Sure enough, we were.

In 1983 when John Root attended the International Plowing Match outside of Richmond, he re-iterated his concern that landfill soil conditions were going to result in hundreds of thousands of dollars in environmental clean-up costs.

The landfill site was taken over in the late 1980's by Regional Government. The issue of management and landfill sites continue to be contentious today. Steps are being taken to manage landfill sites in an environmentally-sensitive way. Locally, hundreds of thousands of dollars have been spent to prevent the migration of groundwater containing leachate away from the site by installing liners and pipes on the landfill site. Leachate is a little like an environmental stew, created when residues are mixed from items such as battery acid, pesticides, paints, pills – that find their way to the landfill. Some citizens throw these items into the garbage instead of disposing of them at the special household hazardous waste site at the landfill site or the one-day depots.

Technological intervention is required; otherwise, left unchecked, this toxic stew can permeate into the ground and eventually find its way into streams and rivers – the source of our drinking water. At last count, eight truck loads a day of leachate were being trucked to the Robert E. Pickard Centre, a sewage treatment plant, for processing, treatment and eventual disposal into the Ottawa River.

Plans to construct a pipeline to transport the leachate using a route through Heart's Desire were appealed to the OMB. One of the plans was to pipe it west to Eagleson Road in Kanata to a pumping station and on to ROPEC at Green's Creek. Five or six farmers opposed that route. Only one urban person supported us – Vickie Mason. Former Regional Councillor Molly McGoldrick-Larsen also provided us with some help. She did everything she could to help us defend our position.

Quality Affordable Health Care

Ontario Premier Bill Davis, left, assisted by Aubrey Moodie, officially opened the Queensway-Carleton Hospital on October 5, 1976.

Following the annexation by Ottawa, Nepean Township re-established a Board of Health which consisted of Reeve Keenan, Dr. A. Howard MacCordick and me. With the expanding population, we saw the requirement for broader services that could only be offered by a county-based health unit, a concern that was shared by the Township of Gloucester. We needed to serve a larger population base to meet provincial criteria required to establish a county health unit. We met our immediate local needs by establishing the Gloucester-Nepean Health Unit on September 1, 1958 at 1547 Merivale Road, next to our new fire station. We worked hard to encourage other communities such as Richmond, South March, and Stittsville to join us. We succeeded. Carleton County took over jurisdictional responsibilities and the Carleton County Board of Health came into being on September 1, 1964.

Building a hospital in Nepean was not only a dream, it was a necessity driven by the postwar baby boom. Nepean residents who needed any type of medical attention were obliged to go to a hospital in Ottawa and at times, were placed on waiting lists. Patients from Nepean, like all other residents in the County of Carleton, paid a daily non-resident fee of $1 up until that requirement was rescinded by the Province in1958. We also had a problem convincing doctors to live in Nepean because residency requirements would prevent them from operating in hospitals in Ottawa.

More than one attempt was made to establish a hospital in Nepean. During the 1950's Richard A. Bell and a group of citizens sought the support of Carleton County Council to construct a hospital where Bell High School is located in Nepean today. Dick Bell and a large delegation made a great presentation to Carleton County Council. Many, many meetings were held and when Bert Lawrence became the Minister of Health, we were confident because he was a resident of the west end. He turned down the request.

In the earlier 1960's, we felt it was time to redouble our efforts to construct a hospital in Nepean so Nepean Township Council appointed a striking committee consisting of Harold Denman, Alex Carman and others. We needed the support of Carleton County Council. There were some strong feelings. One proponent proclaimed that councillors who didn't support the bid would be dealt with at the next municipal election. Carleton Council wasn't impressed with the veiled threat but it did approve the request and committed to help finance the hospital. The Province approved the project in 1966 and the letters patent were issued on November 14, 1966. I was on the first board of directors and continue to be involved to this day – as honourary director.

The first annual general meeting of the hospital was held on November 7, 1968 in the Carleton County Council Chambers. A fund-raising committee, headed by Kay Ryan was formed to raise $4 million. The Chairman, Arnold Keehner of Minto Construction, and the Board of Directors were thwarted in their fundraising efforts then, partly because the Province of Ontario froze hospital funding and partly because of the reorganization of Carleton into Regional Government.

I was asked to serve as Chair of the Board in 1970. I said yes on the basis that if I didn't have a construction commitment from Ontario within two years, I would step down. It was imperative that we meet with Premier Davis. I appointed what I thought was a very strong committee – Dick Bell, Jean Pigott who was Chair of the District Health Council, Harold Denman, Alex Carman and others. A tremendous amount of work went into researching and preparing a brief to substantiate our needs.

We met with Premier Davis in his office in Toronto. He asked, "Why are you here?" I replied, "Mr. Premier, you have our brief. If you have any questions sir, we have a committee here to answer them." He turned to Jean Pigott and called her by her first name, "Jean, do you have any objections to this hospital proceeding?" She said, "None whatsoever, Mr. Premier." He turned to me and called me by my first name, "Aubrey, your hospital is approved." Years later, Jean told me she had been interviewed by the Premier before our meeting and provided him with the background. You have to give Jean credit for her contribution. If it hadn't been for her remarks, the hospital would not have been approved.

Next, we appointed an architect, had the drawings approved and secured the land. In 1974, we negotiated a long-term lease for 50 acres of land with the National Capital Commission. Our vision was to build a hospital, some doctors' offices, and a senior citizens' building on the site. We proposed to locate parking on land north of Tubman's Funeral Home. Residents in nearby Qualicum strongly objected to the parking provision, so that ended the plan for a multi-use site.

Ontario was prepared to provide funding to construct the hospital but we needed to supplement it with local fund raising. When we had reached 50% of our goal, I went with Tom Assaly to see Irving Greenberg of Minto. Irving turned to Tom and asked, "If I give $50,000, what are you going to commit?" Tom Assaly replied, "I will give $25,000." I raised a lot of money because I was in a position where I knew many people. Those were the days when Russ Jackson, the Ottawa Rough Rider quarterback, was an honorary chairman. Mike Anka was a big help to the Queensway-Carleton Hospital's fundraising campaign. I enlisted Mike's assistance to ask his nephew and Ottawa-born star and singer Paul Anka to perform. It was a great performance and a very successful fund raiser.

One of the lessons we learned in one particular effort was to confirm consultants' fundraising fees. I remember how shocked and disappointed Kay Ryan was when the consultants' invoice was presented.

The Queensway-Carleton Hospital (QCH) was opened officially on October 5, 1976 by Premier Bill Davis. As a guest speaker, I had the opportunity to make a casual reference about the future of the hospital. I said, "Mr. Premier, I hope you will take a look at the grounds surrounding this hospital and what they may mean in the future." The Premier quickly retorted, "Aubrey is already making plans to expand the hospital!"

The construction of the QCH was one of my greatest successes. I stepped down as Chair in 1977 and continued as a member of the Board of Directors until 1982.

Since then, I have served as an honorary director, attending as many meetings as I can. Irving Greenberg took over the fund-raising efforts. I have seen many changes over the years and continue to support health care. I believe, however, that procedural and administrative procedures need to be standardized and communicated in the interest of making public institutions including hospital boards more accountable to the public they serve. I have pursued several procedural issues with some success such as: the availability of audited financial statements to corporation members in advance of the annual general meeting; the introduction of a conflict of interest clause covering any contract; and the re-imbursement of monies paid in error in lease agreements for municipal taxes – in the order of $60,000.

Lest you begin to think my loyalty to the QCH is waning, nothing can be further from the truth. I am taking the time to express my views on how we can make improvements because I care deeply about the quality of health care and the judicious use of public funds. As recently as October 11, 2002, I wrote to Premier Ernie Eves to support the QCH's expansion plans. It's an important hospital because it serves almost 400,000 residents of the former municipalities of Nepean, Kanata, Rideau, Goulbourn and West Carleton as well as residents living in the west end of the Ottawa Valley.

The Queensway-Carleton Hospital has undergone some extensive changes thanks to community fundraising drives and grants from the Ontario Government. The $12.8 million provincial grant in 2001-2002 helped expedite the new state of the art childbirth centre which is now open and the CT scan. We received some good news in early 2003 when the Province provided $22 million to the QCH to support the second phase which is expected to be completed by the end of 2004. It will consist of a three-story addition to accommodate emergency, ambulatory care programs, a new main entrance, a 12-bed intensive care unit, a 34-bed medicine unit and a combined 15-bed rehabilitation/23 bed medicine inpatient unit. The second phase includes a two-storey addition to expand diagnostic imaging including the new MRI – the QCH was one of three Ontario hospitals to receive an additional $1.6 million to fund an MRI. A third expansion to be completed in 2006 will include two new operating rooms, expanded ambulatory care services space, three new mental health beds and enhancements of cardiopulmonary, pharmacy, rehabilitation and support services.

The lease doesn't come up for renewal until 2013. One would expect the extension of the lease will protect the integrity of this multi-million investment.

The Board of Directors has some continuing financial challenges to face even though Province of Ontario allocates the largest portion of tax dollars to fund health care. I believe that we can stretch those tax dollars by adopting a number of actions.

When the Queensway-Carleton Hospital celebrated its 20th anniversary, I was asked and agreed to serve as the Honorary Chair of the Ray of Hope Hospital Fund-raising Campaign.

It would be very helpful if the Province of Ontario were to appoint independent auditors, for a maximum of two three-year terms, to audit all public institutions including hospitals and their partners and associated foundations.

I also believe that clear roles and responsibilities must be established between hospital boards and staff and in particular, the delegation of authority and the reporting mechanisms to help the Board of Directors fulfill the fiduciary role and stewardship responsibilities.

Public institutions should model bylaws and policies dealing with issues such as rules of procedure and conflict of interest in accordance with those set by the Ontario Government so the rules are consistent from public agency to public agency and transparent to the taxpayer.

Attracting and keeping qualified people as board members is critical to the success of the hospital and like fundraising, the competition for volunteers is great. I am very impressed with the work board director Mary Pitt has completed as Chair of the Nominating Committee. The entire process has been reviewed and a wider net is being cast to attract proficient and experienced candidates to the Board. It is a very open process which I am confident will produce some excellent results.

The Queensway-Carleton Hospital's newest web site has now gone live. It is one way to keep in touch with the community by posting board agendas, minutes, bylaws, important policies and initiatives to help keep citizens informed of the progress. That's what good public relations is all about.

My work with the Queensway-Carleton Hospital covers a half century. The public was very generous in its financial support of the hospital in its early days, a spirit that continues today. Our partner, the Province of Ontario continues to fund health care as its number one priority. We need to ensure that the use of every dollar is maximized.

A Moodie Memory

Early one evening, in the spring of 1963, I tied my Siamese cat on the front steps. He had an irritating habit of hissing at everything. A passing cat took exception. I mistakenly thought I could prevent a confrontation by opening the door and snatching my cat. The attacking cat overshot his mark and attached himself to my hand. As he would not let go, a fair bit of damage was done.

We proceeded to the Civic Hospital as my hand had doubled in size very quickly. The Civic had a policy that prohibited treating cat bites until they knew if the cat had its rabies shot. I was sent home untreated. By this time, my hand and my arm had tripled in size. All the medical offices were closed. We didn't know what to do so we called the Reeve, Aubrey Moodie, whom I had never met. He listened and then said there would be someone there to help me in a few minutes. A policeman arrived shortly and escorted us back to the Civic. A Nepean health official had arranged for me to be met and treated.

Mr. Moodie telephoned the following day to enquire how I was and to tell me that the police had located the offending cat and determined that it had had its rabies shot.

I look back at a time when Nepean's population was 14,500. Many things have changed, but I don't believe Mr. Moodie has changed from the people person he was 35 years ago.

Jane Corbett

Fishing has been a great form of relaxation for me over the years. My largest catch was a gray trout caught in Great Slave Lake.

$\mathcal{I}$enjoyed many fishing and hunting trips as a charter member of the Carleton Fish and Game Club. On one trip to Great Slave Lake, organized by Ken Hughes who owns the Bells Corners Trailer Park, we had caught our quota of fish. Some of the group wanted to go back on the lake. The waves were getting pretty rough so I returned to the camp. All but two fishermen followed me back. The two, who decided to go out on the lake, were halfway across when they were driven back by the waves. They barely survived the ordeal. I am quite sure had I not refused to venture out on the lake, some of us may have drowned that day.

The first and only time I saw an iceberg was on our trip to Greenland. What a magnificent site.

My "fishing" boat is pictured above and my brother Clifford is in the foreground of the photo to the right.

On another trip to Ungava Bay, we had one group coming in and another leaving. The departing group decided to send its luggage out first. The only problem was fog set in and we couldn't get out for two to three days. It was an awkward situation because we did not have enough food for the two groups and the cook had suffered a heart attack. We shot a caribou and caught fish to survive.

A group from Richmond, including Ralph Thompson and Herb Stinson, hunted at Red Horse Lake, just north of Ompah. We had to portage three miles to get to the camp. It was not fit to live in when we first arrived, so we rebuilt it and called it Tin Cup Camp. We had some great times for six or seven years running deer with the help of a blue speckled hound I bought from Harold Nesbitt. We decided to pack it in because we were getting older and we had experienced a run of bad luck. One of our group got lost in the bush. It was frightening because it took us a quite a while to find him even after we resorted to firing shots into the air. Shortly after, he was cleaning his rifle when it was accidentally discharged. The bullet went through the cabin. One of us could have been injured or killed.

Celebrating a Lifetime Together

On September 12, 1998, the City of Nepean honoured Ella and me by hosting a Tribute to Mr. and Mrs. Nepean on the occasion of our 90th birthdays and our 65th wedding anniversary.

On September 12, 1998, Ella and I were honoured by the City of Nepean on the occasion of our 90th birthdays and our 65th wedding anniversary. Called a Tribute to Mr. and Mrs. Nepean, we were joined by many friends and neighbours.

Nepean citizens and businesses have been served by four heads of Council since 1954: Aubrey Moodie 1954-1969; Mary Pitt 1997-2000; Ben Franklin 1978 to 1997 and Andy Haydon from 1970-1978. Ella Moodie is in the front.

We were joined by hundreds of well wishers including David Pratt, MP for Nepean-Carleton, John Baird, MPP for Nepean, Mayor Mary Pitt, former Mayor Ben Franklin and former Regional Chair, Nepean Reeve and Mayor Andy Haydon. It was a delightful afternoon organized by Councillor Margaret Rywak with help from many citizens and city staff.

Councillor Margaret Rywak, on the right, worked hard as the Chair of the Organizing Committee for this wonderful event.

Presentations were made by Barbara Farber, Councillor Wayne Phillips who was also the former Chief of Police, retired Nepean Police Chief Gus Wersch and Councillor Margaret Rywak. Guest speaker was CJOH's Leigh Chapple. The Country Aires: Peggy and George Tessier performed as did Gospel Grass with Al Spears.

The story is best told by sharing some of the kind expressions of warmth and photographs taken on September 12, 1998 with you. Some of the stories that were given to Ella and me in a commemorative binder appear in this book. I hope you enjoy them as much as I did. They are vignettes of every day concerns that each of us experience.

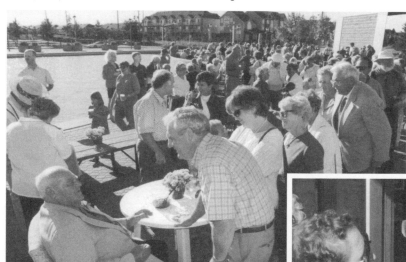

Hundreds of our friends joined us in a celebration at Nepean City Hall, Ben Franklin Place, 101 Centrepointe Drive.

At left, long-time friend and neighbour John Monaghan presented Ella with a bouquet of roses.

Prayer of Thanksgiving

offered by Reverend Grant Dillenbeck, Bells Corners United Church,
at the tribute to Mr. and Mrs. Nepean

Thank you, God, thank you. These words come so easily to our lips, that sometimes, O God, we may be tempted to say them without giving adequate thought to the depth of their meaning. But not today, for today as we say thank you for the blessings we have received from your servants, Aubrey and Ella Moodie, we are completely sincere in our heartfelt gratitude to you, and our genuine appreciation of them.

On this day we honour Ella and Aubrey, recognizing the good number of years they have lived and shared their love in marriage. Yet it has been said that the value of life is best measured, not in terms of the number of years lived, but the number of lives touched, and by this standard, O God, you have so gifted Aubrey and Ella, that their lives are indeed measured as being full to the brim and overflowing. Each of us has been inspired by their devotion to one another, their love of family, the support of the ministry of the church, and their dedication to our community. Everyone here, as well as countless others, has benefited from their guidance, their labours, and their service.

We ask, gracious God, that you will continue to bless Aubrey and Ella with health, compassion and wisdom. That we might still benefit from the richness of their lives for years to come, for we are now and always will be, most fortunate for having the opportunity of sharing our lives with them.

Merciful God, help each of us to seek, by Ella and Aubrey's example, to make a constructive contribution to the welfare of our community, to renew our commitments to family and friends, and to be reminded of your constant loving kindness to us.

And so once more, we offer you these words of gratitude, and I invite everyone gathered here to repeat them after me. Thank you. Thank you.

We ask these prayers in the name of our Lord Jesus Christ, who taught us when praying to say, "Our Father, who art in heaven, hallowed be thy name. Thy kingdom come, thy will be done on earth as it is in heaven. Give us this day our daily bread, and forgive us our trespasses, as we forgive those who trespass against us. And lead us not into temptation, but deliver us from evil. For thine is the kingdom and power and the glory, forever and ever.

Amen.

Going Forward

*A*s I go forward, I don't think that I would do much differently. Today, the emphasis on research and the availability of staff and funding cast an entirely different light on how politicians function. However, there are certain constants that hold true over time:

Surround yourself with talented people: Appoint the proper people to the proper place at the proper time. That's been one of my successes over the years. I had good staff, people like Dave Hobbs. If a good person left the Township and then decided they wanted to return, I would take them back. There were at least two people who returned: Grant Armstrong who went to Osgoode Township and Bud Henry who returned to the Nepean Police Service. You need good staff.

I also worked with many well-qualified Councillors. Ken Kerr, Ed Hall and Hugh McDonald were lawyers and Grant Carman held a Ph.D in agriculture. With few exceptions, I had the support of excellent Councillors.

Own up to your mistakes. I didn't expect to be right all of the time and I never minded people making mistakes, but I never appreciated anyone who wouldn't admit to his or her mistakes.

Be accountable. Elected officials have to be accountable. You are spending taxpayers' hard-earned money. Never forget that.

End the public criticism. Carleton County Council was a close knit group. Not one of us would criticize another council member in public. If we had an issue with another member of Council, the Warden would call Carleton County Council together. Staff would not be present. If after the discussion, the consensus was that the Councillor had erred, he/she would be asked to correct the situation. The Warden would give him/her a lecture. If the member did not accept the decision, his/her participation on committees would be very, very limited. You have to remember, there are very, very few people who don't make some kind of mistake in their lifetime. This way, the lesson is learned without taxpayers incurring the costly burden of law suits.

Elected officials are in charge. There is a new breed of politician and there is more delegation to staff. But Council still sets the policy to govern that delegation of authority. Council has to be in charge and they have to be accountable to citizens.

Independent audits are good for everyone. In my opinion, the appointment of independent auditors for a three year term, by the Province of Ontario for all public institutions, is the only way to verify your tax dollars are spent properly.

Learn the ropes before you jump into the fray. I would encourage citizens to seek election but only if they have the time to learn the ropes first. Don't plan to go too high too fast. You need to get the experience first. You also need to understand the issues before you take a position. If the issue becomes polarized, someone has to backtrack. Otherwise, leadership becomes episodic and the direction is not sustainable. Representing your community is an extraordinary and unforgettable experience depending on how you handle yourself. I, certainly, was never in it for the money.

Respect a person's opinion whether you agree with it or not. That's important if you are going to build solid relationships. You can start by listening to what the person has to say. Don't focus on the person. Focus on the issue he/she is addressing.

Don't be too quick to accept a situation. Very recently, my church was sent a letter from the City of Ottawa advising that the congregation had to refrain from using an access road. We have been using that access road for 40 years and out of the blue, no consultation, no discussion, just a letter! What kind of an approach is that? I conferred with church officials. We now have an agreement with the City and the practice will continue. This may seem like a small detail. There is an important principle. Don't accept things at face value just because it looks official.

There is one more thing... when you are in too deep, pull for time until you can think it through.

Above all, I am blessed with a very loving and supportive wife, the mother of our five children. Our 70th wedding anniversary is coming up in June 2003. I am grateful for the years we have had together.

When you reach my age, you think more about telling your story. There is a stage in your life when you don't. Harry Leikin used to put it this way, "You don't boast your own self." Now, I am more inclined to dwell on the past than the future. You will have to excuse me for that. I have to say something good about the past because it is such a big part of my life. I am now looking for my 95th year and more if I have good health. I hope to be here when I am 103.

INDEX